PRAISE FOR
LIVING YOUR BEST LIFE

"Laura Berman Fortgang will help you reach the success and fulfillment you are destined for."

·KEN BLANCHARD

"Fortgang generously offers glorious, refreshing guidance to help us each find our unique path in life. I scribbled notes on almost every page. I know I will refer to her book over and over again."

·JENNIFER LOUDEN
Author of *The Woman's Comfort Book*
and *The Comfort Queen's Guide to Life*

"Fortgang's Wisdom Access Questions have the makings of brilliance—simple, easy to use, hugely effective, and humblingly obvious. If only we had thought of them first!!"

·JUDY GEORGE
Founder & CEO of Domain
Author of *The Domain Book of Intuitive Home Design*
and *The Intuitive Businesswoman*

"A brilliantly written, indispensable guide that touches and expands the very best of our hearts, minds, and spirits. With fresh insights and practical, powerful exercises, Fortgang shows how to restore and revitalize the precious balance between work and home, life and career, and fulfill our highest destiny."

·HAROLD BLOOMFIELD, M.D.
Author of *Making Peace with Your Past*
and *How to Survive the Loss of a Love*

"Beware—this thought-provoking book will put you on a one-way path to a more creative and fulfilling life. You'll read it cover to cover."

·KYLE MACLACHLAN
actor

"I read Living Your Best Life on a movie set, and everyone kept stealing it from me, reading it while I was shooting, and then raving about it. Finally I got to finish the book and found it amazingly helpful. Laura helps you organize information you already have inside so you can move your life forward in positive ways. I can't recommend this enough!"

·JULIA SWEENEY
actress

LIVING
YOUR
BEST
LIFE

Discover Your Life's
Blueprint for Success

LAURA BERMAN FORTGANG

JEREMY P. TARCHER/PUTNAM
a member of Penguin Putnam Inc.
New York

AUTHOR'S NOTE

Many names and identifying details of the client examples described in this book have been changed to preserve the confidentiality of the coaching relationship.

Most Tarcher/Putnam books are available at special quantity discounts for bulk purchases for sales promotions, premiums, fundraising, and educational needs. Special books or book excerpts also can be created to fit specific needs. For details, write Putnam Special Markets, 375 Hudson Street, New York, NY 10014.

Jeremy P. Tarcher/Putnam
a member of
Penguin Putnam Inc.
375 Hudson Street
New York, NY 10014
www.penguinputnam.com

First paperback edition 2002

The Library of Congress catalogued the hardcover edition as follows:

Fortgang, Laura Berman.
Living your best life : ten strategies for getting from where you
are to where you're meant to be / Laura Berman Fortgang.
p. cm.
ISBN 1-58542-092-1
1. Success—Psychological aspects.   I. Title.
BF637.S8 F635   2001   00-068281
158.1—dc21
Printed in the United States of America

ISBN 1-58542-157-X (paperback edition)

1   3   5   7   9   10   8   6   4   2

Book design by Tanya Maiboroda

This book is dedicated

to Mark,
the wisest man I know,
whose love is my rock,

and

to Skyler,
a chip off his dad's block,
who makes my heart sing

CONTENTS

INTRODUCTION: EXCAVATING YOUR LIFE BLUEPRINT

BECOMING A COACH

The woman in the white jacket looked over my questionnaire. "We'd like to admit you," she said. I was twenty-nine years old and on the verge of becoming a resident patient at Fair Oaks Hospital in Summit, New Jersey, to receive treatment for severe depression and suicidal tendencies. "No, that won't be necessary," I replied through nervous laughter as I got up to leave.

They let me go. They didn't even try to stop me. Maybe it was the certainty with which I responded or maybe it was because they had planned to scare me straight. Whichever, it did not matter. All that *did* matter is that in that moment something shifted in me forever. I decided to turn my life around. I decided to find a way out from behind what I had taken to calling the "black curtain." I decided that I could change, that I did not have to be "a very sick girl," as my family and doctors said I was.

At that moment, something stronger than I was took over and directed me down a path I had no idea whether I could follow. Over the preceding six years I had weathered depression, pain, and a life that did not work, but now I did not know if I could cope with healing, forgiveness, and happiness.

My previous years of on-and-off-again therapy had not made a big impact, although I had been the most entertaining patient a shrink could find. Mine should have been paying me for my weekly stand-up comedy routine, which included an occasional Sarah Bernhardt impersonation. After D day at the hospital, I tried a little more therapy. I even tried antidepressants. At the time, nothing seemed more enticing to me than a little magic pill to lighten the leadlike heaviness I felt running through my veins and brain. But five days after starting the pills, I was on the StairMaster and suddenly could not breathe. I thought I was having a heart attack. When my pulse came down, I was fine, but I took this incident as a sign that drugs were not going to free me of my problems. I quit Zoloft. I knew I had to figure this thing out on my own.

Predating all this was a long struggle with anorexia and exercise bulimia. My every day had been centered around what I would eat, when I would eat it, and when I could work out to burn off the calories I had consumed.

Ninety-five pounds and zero percent body fat looked great to me. My eyes were like marbles because there were no cheeks to surround them. My knees were knobby like hammers and my hip bones darted out like the fins on a 1950s Cadillac. Like all anorexics, I was proud, not worried about my health at all, and sure that those looks people darted at me were jealousy over my perfect form. Yet, one day, I found myself wishing for a stranger to come and take me off the StairMaster so I could rest. Realizing that somewhere, down deep, I was crying for help, I had a flash of understanding that something was really wrong.

The frenzy that I had worked myself into had to do with a personal characteristic that has always been both my greatest strength and my most dangerous weakness: my drive to succeed. Right after college, I had decided that no matter what it took, I would become an actress. I wanted to be sure I would not, one day, regret not having gone for my dream. But being a poor, struggling artist was not an option. So I earned half of my income from acting and the rest from waitressing, aerobics instructing, shoe modeling, and anything else you could do with your clothes on. I'd wait on line for auditions as early as five A.M., then pound the pavements pursuing acting jobs until three P.M., when I'd take a power nap before waitressing from four to midnight. I was miserable, and yet I thought this lifestyle was leading me somewhere. I was sure I had all the answers to life and that I was somehow superior to others because I was taking action—lots and lots of action—instead of just passively letting life happen.

The only place I did not seek perfection was in romantic relationships. I wanted desperately to be loved, and I had hardly any criteria as to whom I'd allow to do so. When I think back on the many near misses and stupid capers that I put myself through, I realize that I am lucky to be alive. I really can't bring myself to reveal what my mistakes were, but I will say that I hope my kids grow up to have more self-esteem than I did at the time. I hope they know how to say no and mean it. Most of these stunts you could write off as the stupid stuff you do when you're in your twenties. But when I got involved with a married, gun-peddling drug dealer, I realized I had crossed the line from stupid to self-destructive.

It is ironic that, a few years later, the event that finally cracked me open like an egg was a marriage proposal from my beloved boyfriend, Mark. Mark was a penniless actor with no prospects, and because he did not match the "a man will take care of you" myth that I had grown up with, my brain went haywire. Something did not compute. I knew no one had ever loved me like Mark did and yet the perfectionist in me could not settle for someone less than perfect. Shortly afterward, I ended up at the door of Fair Oaks.

I was awful to Mark. I broke off our relationship in a terrible way. I guess it is fair to say that I landed in the hospital because somebody dared to love me. Everything I thought I was, every belief I had, could no longer hold true under the power of having to be vulnerable in the face of love and intimacy.

"A Course in Miracles," a self-study psycho-spiritual course, says: "Love brings up all unlike itself." Well, there was a lot of "unlike" in me and it all came pouring out. Every illusion, every assumption about how life worked was up for grabs and I crashed like a crystal chandelier falling from a cathedral ceiling. All the while, Mark stood by me.

The worst three years of my life—eighteen months of a borderline ability to function, howling hysterically every day, followed by eighteen months of fragile rebuilding—is one of the things I am most grateful for having experienced. Thanks to those years, I was humbled, I grew up, and I developed compassion for myself and for other human beings. I let go of the illusion that I had control over everything in my life, and I began to hear the voice of my own inner wisdom instead of those perfectionistic demons. I had hurt myself so badly striving for some fabricated ideal that I now made a pact with myself and some power greater than me in order to move on. I called my pact "Happiness, Peace, and Love." I know it sounds corny, but I decided that if those three things were truly my priorities, how many pounds I weighed and what I did for a living and how much money my fiancé had were of no real consequence. (Yes, I married him.) After that defining moment at the hospital, I decided I wanted to learn how to live, and I set out to teach myself how to have happiness, peace, and love.

Soon after, I had an intuitive inkling to call an old acquaintance. Out of nowhere, I had gotten the feeling that he could give me a job or help me find a new line of work, which was what I needed while rebuilding my world. That inkling became a nagging, and after a week of trying to ignore it, I dialed his number. Jay had become a personal coach, a success partner who spoke weekly to those in a career change or life transition, to guide them with ideas and encouragement and hold them accountable to the new life they wanted to create. We agreed that becoming his client would be a fine way for me to decide what was next on my career and life path.

I worked with Jay for a year and a half to build a small presentation-skill-training business, which married my acting background with the corporate world. As I worked with people to bring out their public-speaking best, I realized I was having more of an impact on them than just telling them in what position to hold their hands while talking or how to craft an attention-getting opening to their speech. I had become a coach. I was helping others carve out what was great about them and then leverage it into a more fulfilling life. After working with Jay, I completed two years of coach training while starting my practice, and knew I had now found what I was meant to do.

I quickly went from coaching actors who could barely pay me $50 a month to being "discovered" in a *Money* magazine article, which featured a client whom I had coached to raise her income to $500,000. I soon found myself in a bidding war between two companies who wanted to publish my first book. Only five years passed from the last time I wore my waitressing Reeboks to the day in 1998 when I held in my hands the first printed copy of the result, *Take Yourself to the Top.* That journey had its up and downs, but for the most part it was effortless. I did not plan it, anticipate it, control it, or even, for that matter, seek it out.

Considering my history, that must be hard to believe. But it's true. My last words to my old career were "If big success is meant to be, it will come find me." And find me it did. I met up with my path by using the magic of doing what felt right, taking care of my financial and emotional needs, and letting the rest unfold as it would. It is that magic that I would like to see in everybody else's life.

As a coach, I have helped people start and grow businesses, move up the corporate ladder, improve the quality of their lives, and feel more satisfied overall. Although I have been known for creating results in careers, small businesses, and large corporations, I've never quite felt that being called a business coach or a career coach said it all. What I consider myself to be is a life coach. The people I've helped achieve success have ranged across ages, races, income brackets, and industries, yet the way I've worked with them to get the results they craved has little to do with my expertise in business. Rather, it has to do with my belief that we each have a built-in blueprint for our lives within us. This blueprint describes our "best life," the life we are meant to live, the life that will bring us the most happiness and satisfaction with the least effort. It is that blueprint I would like to help you discover.

LIFE BLUEPRINTS

A life blueprint infers that there is a plan for your life. I believe there is one and it is up to you whether you want to participate in it or not. It's up to you if you'd like admission to the movie of your life—the one with the happy ending. This blueprint is not a rigid, predestined, one-option-only plan, but rather a structure from which to create the future of your choice. It's a structure that holds the clues to comfort and happiness in your own skin and the path to your best life.

Without help, though, we're often unable to see this best life. So we cling to conventional models of achieving success, such as what we see our friends and coworkers doing and the messages the media send. We work hard; we schmooze the boss; we try to be super parents; we try to be good. Striving in these ways makes us feel that we're working toward something productive, but it also ultimately makes us feel that we are chasing our tails: doing more to be "successful" so that we can earn our time to relax and enjoy—a time that never seems to come.

A much easier way to "have it all" is within our grasp, however. When we learn to see our life blueprint, we can structure our lives according to that deep-seated plan, so that we can find the most *organic* version of our personal and professional success. This means not just being happy and successful, but living a life in which these good things come to you easily, without the stress, strain, strife, or effort that you may have come to accept as a "normal" part of life. Being happy doesn't have to be hard!

Reaching a state of ease is what the journey you will take with me as your coach is all about. You will work to get to a point where your life "clicks." No one will have to tell you when that happens—you'll know your life is clicking because you'll have nothing to complain about. Boring, right? Well, as Thomas Leonard, an early mentor of mine, used to say, "Boredom is the gateway to inner peace."

So how do we learn to identify our best life? How do we reach the most organic version of our success? It involves becoming able to listen to a wisdom that we all have within us, a wisdom for which we are innately wired, a wisdom that holds the answers to our quest for satisfaction in life. Learning to access and apply that wisdom is how we will reach the ease and satisfaction I am promising.

Living Your Best Life is not intended to be a prescription for overcoming anorexia or mental illness. I share my personal battle with such problems in these pages because I hope my own experience serves as a metaphor for whatever personal and professional obstacles you may be facing in your life. Using my skills as a life coach, in the following pages I will take you through a process that will help you overcome any obstacles that lie between you and your best life. This process will take you within, instead of looking outward to the model or rules of others for solutions. By using what is within you—your own wisdom—you will save time, energy, and money. You'll stop doing umpteen million things in pursuit of what you believe you want, and instead you'll unleash your innate wisdom and allow your built-in extraordinary life to evolve as it's meant to.

Whether you are a corporate executive or an entrepreneur, a Generation X-er or a homemaker, as your life coach I will help you get in touch with who you really are and what you really want. I will help reflect your inner wisdom outward, where you can hear it. Through this book, I'll give you the support, permission (many of us need it), and a clear structure through which to follow that wisdom to successes that might ordinarily be beyond your wildest dreams.

For example, you'll read about Michelle, who had always done everything "right" in her life—including sticking to the career path she had chosen, despite her desire to follow a new interest she loved. You'll see how she began to trust what was true for her and as a result found her way into her dream career. You'll also meet Dianne, a homemaker who finally overcame her tendency to take care of others before herself and was freed to reclaim a position of strength in her marriage and in her dealings with a friend who was taking advantage of her talents. These changes led her to a new sideline as a documentary filmmaker. You'll also get to meet Rick, who shed a series of circumstances that made him miserable and moved to New York for a new, exciting job. This was a dream he did not think was possible until he learned through coaching how to take action on the answers to his happiness, which he already possessed.

An extraordinary future is yours for the taking, and we will unlock the door to your best life by paying more attention to who you are than to what you do. I'll show you how to take responsibility for the circumstances of your life, which will free you to be yourself—something that leads to extraordinary outer changes in your world. As you evolve, your life improves. As a result, your interest in step-by-step goals with their linear emphasis on getting this or that, will start to fall by the wayside; in their stead, you will develop an understanding of what coaching does: it enables you to create the conditions in your world so that great luck can find you. As you read this book, I'd like you to imagine that we are working on an archaeological dig. With me as your coach, we will brush away the dust from your life in order to allow its outline, the blueprint for your best life, to come to the surface.

HOW TO EXCAVATE
YOUR LIFE BLUEPRINT

This book will take you through three stages of blueprint excavation, which I have affectionately named the Reckoning, the Doing, and the Being. Much like any archaeological excavation, the bones and other findings (the Reckoning) are only the beginning. The other stages serve to put the bones together and allow what was supposed to be, and once was, to be again.

- **The Reckoning** is a very necessary first stage. It helps bring forth the more productive thinking that will get you what you want.
- **The Doing** aids you in understanding the physical actions you need to take in order to create the life circumstances that breed success and fulfillment.

■ **The Being** introduces you to the real magic in life. It helps you stretch so that you can tap those spiritual resources that will help you learn how to set up your life to receive the unexpected. This stage also assists you in recognizing signs that your wisdom is trying to guide you.

As you move through the three stages, you'll work through ten strategies, each the focus of one of the chapters of this book:

1. *Ask What, Not Why*
   In this first strategy, you'll learn the questions that can help you begin to move forward. These questions are the root of my success with clients.

2. *Train the Brain*
   Here, you'll learn how to train your brain to recognize any negative beliefs you may be holding.

3. *Gain Perspective*
   I'll show you how you can gain a clearer perspective on yourself and move through work and life challenges more quickly and easily.

4. *Act on What You Feel, Not on What You Think*
   This strategy will help you make the transition from thinking to action.

5. *Make a Simple Contract*
   To get off the treadmill of compensating for present circumstances, you will make what I call a "simple contract" with yourself to get every part of your life to work.

6. *Discover Your Lucrative Purpose*
   Understanding the hidden messages in your dreams and aspirations will show you your lucrative purpose in life, both financially and in terms of even greater riches.

7. *Make Yourself a Magnet*
   There are conditions that repel or attract good things to you, and this step shows you how to make the laws of magnetism work to your benefit.

8. *Become a Master at Focusing*
   Here, you make the transition from action to its best-life chemistry partner, being.

9. *Ask for Directions Before You Are Lost*
   This strategy presents simple ways to make your own intuition something you can easily tap into and depend on for guidance and for fulfilling solutions to your life queries.

10. *Give Up Needing to Know*
    In the final strategy you give up the need to be certain of an outcome before you take action or follow a hunch.

For this program to achieve its maximum impact, I suggest you work through all of these strategies in order. There is a logic to their sequence. Nevertheless, if you jump around out of order or focus on only one or two strategies, they will still work for you. If you feel "stuck" at any point, go back to earlier steps and restudy the strategies that seem to touch on what is most troublesome for you. For example, if you find yourself in the Doing section working on your simple contract, but you cannot "get over" blaming what is wrong or missing what is lacking in your life, you'll need to revisit the Reckoning section and engage in those exercises again.

If any element of my program causes you emotional upheaval, do find the support you need. In my coaching company, my associates and I sometimes recommend that a client work with a licensed counselor. Therapy heals the past, coaching designs the future, so if the past is a problem, please take care of it.

By the same token, you may find you're more comfortable in one of the three stages more than the others. For example, those who are highly analytical, skilled at unraveling complicated situations, and perhaps need to justify or have answers for everything are likely to relate very naturally to the Reckoning. If you are immersed in worldly pursuits, in maneuvering deals, and in working nonstop, but you still feel unsatisfied, you are probably innately well versed in the Doing; like my client Mitch, whom you'll read about in Part Two, you know how to make your life function; it just may be tiring and stressful and somewhat out of balance. If you have a hard time making concrete parts of your life work, you may be already very spiritually developed and open to the Being; even the most enlightened beings can have financial problems if they have not gained worldly wisdom, too.

Working across all three of these stages, not just the one in which you are most comfortable, is key to discovering your blueprint: your peace of mind and ease of accomplishment.

Although I am coaching you through this book, you may wish to develop a live coaching relationship with a professional coach or by teaming up with a partner, friend, or a small group. There are instructions on how to form your own blueprint group in Appendix 4.

EXCAVATING YOUR LIFE BLUEPRINT— THE TOOLS

I believe the idea of "gaining" wisdom is a bit of a misnomer. As I see it, wisdom is the memory of the soul. It is the source of the meaning, purpose and satisfaction that so many of us are waiting for. We don't so much gain wisdom as we lose along the way what wisdom we were born with. It then becomes our task to uncover it underneath all the cultural and experiential baggage that has kept us from finding it.

If you use this book well, you'll start to recognize truths that you know but had forgotten, as well as lessons that you didn't even realize you had learned. You'll drop the habits that have kept you from hearing the internal promptings that have the power to positively guide the course of your life. You'll gain the tools to bring to the surface the things you already deeply know, and the courage to put these insights into action.

As I guide you through the three stages of excavating your life blueprint, I will give you these tools. They include:

Wisdom Access Questions, or WAQs. In chapter 1, "Ask What, Not Why," I will explain what a Wisdom Access Question is and how to use WAQs to begin the process of living your best life. You will move from "why" questions, which ask for a reason, to "what" questions, which help you, in the first stages of your excavation, examine what is wrong or missing in your life and then pinpoint ways to solve the problem. You'll be asked to use these kinds of questions throughout this book.

Wisdom in Action. These exercises will help crystallize what you are learning during each of the three stages of discovering your best life. They will have the most impact if performed right when you first read them; however, if you choose to return to the exercises later, that is fine, too. The important thing is to do them, because coaching works from the actions you take, not just the awareness you gain. You may want to practice Wisdom in Action exercises a number of times in areas of the program where you feel you are stuck.

Wisdom Writing. Sometimes I'll ask you to find out more about yourself by writing. Wisdom Writing can help access your own wisdom, which may have been hiding in the crevices of your highly analytical mind or in that part of your mind that fell asleep with your dreams many years ago. Create a file in your computer for this work or buy a notebook or journal to use just for this project.

Wisdom Stories. The experiences of many of my clients and workshop participants will bring to life the work we are doing together.

This book is designed to give you step-by-step work that produces immediate results. You may wish you had done it sooner, but don't waste energy on regrets. Take your time, and you'll learn how to get from where you are to where you are meant to be—happily living your best life.

PART ONE

THE RECKONING

DURING THE COURSE OF A NORMAL DAY WE HAVE ABOUT sixty thousand thoughts,* many of which come and go so quickly that we are not even aware of them. Some of these thoughts may set us up to "win" in life. But how many of our thoughts keep us from our potential? That is a question only you can answer, and each nonproductive thought is an impediment to your personal fulfillment only you can change.

I had never placed much stock in those motivational people who tout positive thinking. But I learned the value of their message as soon as I had no other choice in my life but to change what I was thinking, one thought at a time, in order to turn my life around. Even today, I still bristle at folks who sound overly positive, because I know real life has its inevitable ebbs and flows. In my view—and, I assume, in yours—it's a sign of maturity when a person can admit to having all the shades of emotions humans experience. Therefore, I'm not going to throw the-power-of-positive-thinking rhetoric your way. What I will do in the following chapters is walk you through very practical ways in which you can use your mind to access your life blueprint more quickly, in order to then lead you to your best life.

The Reckoning is the first stage in excavating and then reconstructing your life blueprint. To live up to the life you were meant to lead, you must begin by looking at what has shackled you and prevented you from hearing your own inner voice of wisdom. When you reckon, you are able to understand why you may be seeing the world in a less than productive way. The main task of the Reckoning is not to understand the influence the past has had on your life (again I leave that to psychotherapists), but to give you the tools you need to move forward. The purpose of the Reckoning is to help you "get over yourself": you have to accept that you have what you have, you are what you are, your parents did what they did, and you still deserve to have an extraordinary life.

When you work through this first stage of uncovering your blue-

---

*William Reville, from article in the "Science Today" column in *The Irish Times,* May 29, 2000.

print, you are making a commitment to overcoming the biggest obstacle to most people's attainment of satisfaction with their lives—themselves. You are committing to overcoming negative self-concepts, limiting beliefs, and bad habits that can get in the way of the wisdom that is trying to lead you to your best life. In the next three chapters, you will learn how to get over these hurdles by asking better questions in order to get better answers to your life's queries; reframing beliefs that stunt your ability to have what you want; and gaining the perspective you need to allow your life's desires to soar.

What happened to a client of mine named Monica shows how the Reckoning can help. Monica wanted desperately for her band to reach the top of the music charts. But her naturally volatile temperament, combined with her fierce determination to make this happen, were working against her. When we began to work together, I told her that if success was indeed part of her ultimate blueprint, some reckoning was needed. She needed to get out of her own way and change the questions she posed. Instead of "Who is responsible for this?," "How dare you speak to me that way?," or "Who does she think she is?," she needed to be asking "What do I want from this situation?," "What would be fair to everyone?," and "What will make the difference to getting more money for the band?" Monica had to gain perspective and realize that not everything that was happening around her was *about* her. She needed to adjust some of the beliefs she held about her worth and how to prove it.

Once she did all this, she was free of the struggle. She decided to move on from her band and to pursue an acting career and a family life. Later, Monica returned to the music business with a completely new band put together in a way that did not compromise her newfound clarity.

What moved Monica from being purely reactive to her world to being on track with her life blueprint is what we will explore for you in the Reckoning. Even if you don't think you have any reckoning to do, work through this part anyway. The exercises in the three chapters that follow will benefit you regardless of whether you think you need them.

Shall we?

ASK WHAT, NOT WHY

R ECKONING WITH YOUR MIND IN ORDER TO FREE UP YOUR
capacity for wisdom is the ongoing battle of life. For some, the
battle is constant; others are not as affected. Regardless of which
category you fall into, this chapter will give you the first tool for accessing the wisdom that can change your life. It's a tool you use every
day: the ordinary, common question.

One of the most common questions we ask is "Why?" "Why" is
the language of seeking to understand. When we were young children, we used this question to figure out how the world works: "Why
is the sky blue?," "Why did Sparky run away?" As we get older, we still
use "why" to bring our circumstances into alignment with our ability
to understand our world.

Unfortunately, "why" eventually loses its power to move us forward; instead, we get "stuck" by obsessing over questions like "Why
did that happen?," "Why am I this way?," and "Why aren't I better-
thinner-smarter?"

Even if you're not in the throes of despair, you might still be
stuck using despair's questions. When you use "why" to ask a question, you are struggling to come up with information to help you
understand a situation or circumstance. I call this asking an information question. Information questions will give you answers that ex-

plain the past. They yield answers that fill the coffers of your mind with details, as well as emotion, blame, and perhaps even more problems. While we assume that more information will enable us to be released from our problems, an information question does little to move you forward in life. In fact, sometimes they can't even be answered. In working with clients for almost a decade, I've seen them endure more frustration than necessary because they asked too many information questions. Asking bad questions is a bad habit.

But don't get me wrong: asking "Why?" has been the key to many a brilliant discovery. When it comes to making changes in our lives, however, "why" is not an effective short-term tool. The way to your life blueprint requires asking deeper, more useful questions in order to get better answers and more effective action. The questions that will help you do that are access questions, which I like to call Wisdom Access Questions. These questions access your innate wisdom to create positive, forward motion.

WISDOM ACCESS QUESTIONS

Imagine your brain as one big Yahoo.com. It is a search engine tapping into a data bank of information that you already have available to you and that is made up of acquired experience, knowledge, and intuition. When you need answers in life, you form questions that serve as your keywords. Your brain then searches its resources and gives out possible answers. The more specific your keyword entry, the more specific your answer—that's the wisdom of the computer. How did it know you needed exactly that? You told it your question and it found the answer for you. This is what Wisdom Access Questions (WAQs) will do—help you be specific in your information gathering so you can come up with answers that have the power to move you forward.

Nearly all the questions we ask begin with one of five words: "who," "what," "why," "when," or "how." Although these words help us gather facts and understand each other in conversation, not all of them yield wisdom. We've already eliminated "why" as a viable Wisdom Access Question. " Who," "when," and "how" fall into the information question category. However, using "what" helps the brain behave as an efficient search engine. "What" questions force you to be specific in your query and being specific leads to solution and awareness; on the other hand, asking "Why?" leaves you with only the question.

For example, if I asked you, "Why are you reading this book?," you might tell me a story about some things you are wondering about. Maybe you'd go on to provide a few details about what brought you to this moment of information seeking. Your responses would probably have something to do with your past. But if I asked, "What outcome do you want to reach by reading this book?," the answer you give would be future-oriented. It would also be much more specific, since you would be forced to look forward, rather than backward. This releases energy and moves you from feeling stuck to living in possibility—you can see opportunities just over the horizon.

So let me ask you again: What outcome do you want to reach by reading this book? Answers like "To get a new life," "To be happier in what I do," or "To find the guts to take a huge risk" have a momentum of their own—regardless of what the final result ends up being, these responses get you moving toward a goal.

The search engine in our brains is highly sophisticated, but it requires a well-phrased question to take advantage of it. WAQs are designed to do that. Using "what" questions provides the opportunity to start you along the road to accessing your own wisdom.

Take a look at the list of questions below and see how you can make any question a Wisdom Access Question by using "what."

CONVERTING INFORMATION QUESTIONS INTO WISDOM ACCESS QUESTIONS

Instead of Asking Yourself:	*Ask:*
Why is this happening to me?	What do I need to get through this?

Why am I such a failure?	What will get me what I want?
Why aren't I better at this?	What can I do to improve?
Why can't I get it?	What do I need to know to understand?
Why can't I have a charmed life like _____?	What can I learn from _____?
Instead of Asking Others:	*Ask:*
Why did she say that?	What could have made her say that?
Whose fault was it?	What is the solution?
Who did what?	What would have made a difference?
What happened? [seeking details]	What happened? [seeking outcome]
Why would they do that?	What could be learned from this?
How will you do that?	What will you do?

See Appendix 2 for additional Wisdom Access Questions.

HOW AND WHEN TO USE WAQS

Imagine two friends commiserating over a problem. One is expressing a complaint and the other is taking the supportive role. If the supporter was to ask information questions—Where were you? Who started it? Why?—he would be treated to details about who did what to whom in a blow-by-blow reenactment of the drama. However, if the supporter knew how to ask Wisdom Access Questions—What is upsetting about what happened?—the friend with the problem would move from problem to solution in record-breaking time.

To find the appropriate "what" question to ask, you must change the focus from details and information to outcomes. Get away from trying to understand a problem and move toward solving it. In the process, you'll see that you don't really need to understand a dilemma to know how to solve it. Using "what" questions will train you to think toward the future, as if you are already ahead of the problem. "What" assumes that a solution is the goal.

Sometimes, we want to be left alone with our problems for a while. Have you ever tried to help a friend who didn't really want help? Remember how frustrated that left you feeling? When you or someone you know wants to mull over a problem, not solve it, all the WAQs in the world are not going to help. You must truly want to stop ruminating and start solving the problem if "what" questions are to be of any use.

Even though you can do this all by yourself, I believe it helps to watch other people gain clarity when you ask them "what" questions. Asking WAQs is a productive and highly generous listening tool for you to use with friends, colleagues, and loved ones. Allowing another person to hear herself is a wonderful gift. This kind of thoughtful communication takes time and patience, but it will improve the quality of the relationship. Whether you use Wisdom Access Questions to move yourself or someone else forward, keep in mind that you have found a great tool.

I use WAQs with my clients, thus enabling them to create more positive circumstances more quickly than they do on their own. My clients predictably begin to experience breakthroughs, both small and large, which I really can't take credit for. I'm just there asking the right question. It's my clients who have the answers—they just needed a prompt in order to accelerate the discovery.

Nothing makes me happier than to hear a client say, "That's a good question." Or better yet, "I hate you for asking me that!" Those are surefire signs that we have struck gold—wisdom.

Let's get question-asking to work for you. If you are ready to begin using WAQs, it may be hard to phrase them properly at first. The two conversations that follow cover the same subject matter but with dramatically different results. In the first, you'll see a coach speak with a client in a more conventional way, without using Wisdom Access Questions.

CLIENT: Something's really bothering me about this decision and I can't quite put my finger on it.

COACH: Why do you think that is?

CLIENT: I don't know. I've been giving it a lot of thought, but nothing's clear.

COACH: Why do you think this is bothering you?

CLIENT: It's something about this guy. . . .

COACH: Was it something he said to you?

CLIENT: Oh, he said he knew these people who could help with the deal and then, when I asked who they were, he avoided giving me names.

COACH: How did that make you feel?

CLIENT: Annoyed.

COACH: Did any one thing annoy you?

CLIENT: Just everything.

COACH: Do you know what you want to do now?

CLIENT: Just drop the whole thing, I think. But I'm just not sure.

The coach's questions asked here focus on information seeking, and in such a nonspecific way that the client isn't prompted to provide dynamic answers that would propel him forward. There is no freedom from the problem, no break from its burden, no movement toward a solution.

Now compare the approach in our next example, where the coach uses WAQs.

CLIENT: Something's really been bothering me about this decision and I can't quite put my finger on it.

COACH: Take a guess—*what* is it that's bugging you?

CLIENT: I don't know.

COACH: If you pretended you knew, *what* would you say?

CLIENT: Hmm. I don't trust the guy who brought me the idea.

COACH: You don't trust the guy. *What* led you to that conclusion?

CLIENT: He has been very vague. He won't commit to anything he has said. I've even asked him about it.

COACH: *What* do you need to move ahead?

CLIENT: I need to find someone I can trust.

COACH: Great. Any ideas as to who?

CLIENT: Yes. There's another guy I think could do the job much better.

COACH: When will you call him?

CLIENT: Today!

Eureka! Clarity, relief, action, forward motion. Here, the client's answers are dynamic and they ring with certainty. Wisdom is attained and, with it, a break from the burden of the problem. This liberating break is the result of using Wisdom Access Questions.

WISDOM IN ACTION

Now it's your turn to practice what you've learned. Spend the next twenty-four hours using WAQs on your job and in your life. Instead of telling someone what to do, ask her a question. Before jumping in to deal with a problem with an employee, ask him, "What do you see that we can do here?" If your teenager is sulking and wallowing in a concern, ask her, "What do you want to see happen in this situation?" If she can answer, then ask another question: "What's the first step?" Keep asking questions until the person you're dealing with comes up with the solution.

Make it clear from the outset of any such conversation that you are trying out something new on them. Keep your tone light and fun, asking, "Do you mind if I ask you some questions, to see if I can help you come up with a solution to your problem?"

Appendix 2 contains an extensive list of sample WAQs. It may help you to have that list in front of you when you do this exercise.

When your twenty-four hours are up, use your journal to record your experiences. Were some conversations better than others? Which ones, and why? Also jot down how you might incorporate WAQs into your life more now that you have experience with them.

USING "WHAT" AS A WAQ

Peggy is a corporate executive who participated in one of my wisdom seminars. She told me about an employee who always saw the glass as half empty, never half full. He found the fault in anything and the negative side of everything. Peggy felt he didn't want to take responsibility for his actions. He justified everything he did by saying it was someone else's fault or someone gave him the wrong information. Peggy struggled with how to get him to see that he was indeed involved and accountable for his own words and actions.

On a recent conference call, Peggy had to deliver some difficult news to her team about significant changes in the company. This employee was on the call and was disruptive and very self-involved. It made her realize she had to address his behavior sooner rather than later.

"What I really wanted to say to him," Peggy told me, "was 'Who do you think you are? Why do you expect me or the company to help you? Why do you always see things in the most negative light? If you spent less time on the phone gossiping, you'd have the time and positive energy to devote to planning and executing for success. And the way to get any positive reinforcement from me, or to get me to embrace the issue as you see it, is not by being passive-aggressive on a conference call, asking me the same question four times, or pushing my hot buttons in an attempt to corner me into a response. Whether you like it or not, I am the manager. You are the representative. This is not a democracy. I will lead and you will follow.'"

Instead, Peggy addressed the issue with her employee in a casual conversation over dinner. She had her notes from my seminar with her, along with a list of WAQs. Here's what she said:

"On our conference call, I picked up on the tension in your voice. Tell me *what* you found upsetting about the new incentive plan. Let me ask that another way. *What* emotion was triggered in you as we discussed the plan? *What* do you want now? *What* is your goal for this year? *What* will get you what you want? *What* can I do to help? *What* can we do together to make it work?"

The employee was bowled over, but also stymied. He'd been expecting Peggy to go for the jugular, but she didn't buy into his crisis. She consciously decided to pull back and once he realized there would be no fight, he was forced to respond in the same way. The Wisdom Access Questions Peggy asked left no room for excuses, self-justification, or any defensive behaviors. He was left with no one to look at but himself. After this frank, open discussion, he and Peggy were aware of his insecurities, his fears, and his goals.

She was able to learn what he wanted from her as his boss because she used WAQs. They diffused a very difficult situation. You saw the raw emotional reaction in her words to me, which anyone could understand and relate to. However, Peggy made a deliberate choice to seek a solution instead of fishing for more information, and getting mired in emotion, blame, and details. In so doing, she was able to improve a working relationship she long ago decided was beyond repair. This was a challenge for Peggy, but in committing to elevating the exchange, she challenged her employee too, and together they got new, unexpected results. Wisdom Access Questions were essential in making this possible.

WAQS AND RELATIONSHIPS

You've seen how Wisdom Access Questions help in a work-related scenario, but they are equally effective in other areas of your life, such as romantic relationships. My friend Scott recently told me how WAQs led him and his wife to have what she said was "one of the best conversations" they'd had in years. His wife had a problem she wanted to discuss, and what Scott had done was resist his natural urge to jump in with a solution. Instead, he talked through the issues involved, using "what" questions only. His wife was able to solve her own problem, thanks in no small part to Scott's attentive questions. She felt connected to him and very loved and supported.

. Scott understood that he did not have to "do" anything for his wife. Nor did he have to "fix" anything for her. Just asking the right questions was the loving listening and helpful support she needed.

Never underestimate the power of a few access questions to raise the level of intimacy in a relationship. When people feel heard and when they are helped to hear themselves, they often experience a deep connection to the power they have. This is often translated into deep gratitude for the person who helped them get there. Whether they are conscious of it or not, this greater sense of connection to oneself and another makes for the kind of relationships most people are looking for.

A CAVEAT

As you begin to realize the benefit of using WAQs in your home and work life, I need to warn you of an exception to the "It's good to ask 'What?'" rule. There is in fact one "what" question that is not a WAQ, but an "information" question. You've probably used it countless times on yourself and on others. Ready?

"What should I do?"

Oh, yes, that's a very big "what" question but definitely not a WAQ. How many times have you asked friends, "What should I do?," or told yourself you "really should" do x, y, or z? The answers to "What should I do?" prevent you from asking the most powerful WAQ you can use. It's very simple and it's the exact opposite: "What do I want?"

That's it. I know it sounds very simple. And very easy. But most people have a really hard time answering this question, because most of us don't know what we want. I see this up close every day. Most smart, sophisticated people, with goals and plans, *think* they know what they want. However, truly having a sense of what would make them happy is a different story. We tend to be much more certain of what we should do, say, wear, or look like than of what will guide us to inner happiness.

It is my experience that seven out of ten people don't really know what they want. They think they do, but they come to discover that much of what drives them is unmet needs or the expectations of others. We will work on making sure you do know what you want in Part Two, but for now just avoid asking the information question "What should I do?"

WISDOM IN ACTION

Start making it a habit to ask yourself, before every conversation, every decision, and every meeting, "What do I want?" For example, if you are about to make a call that makes you anxious, take a minute to figure out what you want to have when that call ends. A job, a sale, an apology, an agreement to revisit the topic if it does not go well?

If you can't answer, take a deep breath and ask again. If the answer still eludes you, explore whether you really want something at all or if you are just reacting to something you've left unsaid or are feeling needy in some way. (I know you'd hate to admit that, but it happens.)

Maybe you really want to finish that argument in a way that feels better or get a raise without having to plead for it. Maybe what you really want is something as simple as a hug. An actor would never walk onstage without knowing why his character is in the scene. By asking "What do I want?" you too will know what you have come to accomplish.

THE POWER OF "WANT" VERSUS "SHOULD"

My phone rang. It was time for Patricia's fourth session with me and, upon picking up the phone, I could instantly hear her agitation. "I've been trying to rewrite my résumé all week and I just can't decide which direction will make it what I want it to be. Should I be focusing on getting a job in advertising or make it read stronger for work in software marketing?"

Patricia was a singer/songwriter by avocation and a successful communications professional in the "real world." She wanted to solidify her plans to find more fulfilling work in the career that paid the bills and, at the same time, further her artistic endeavors. In our earlier sessions, she had said things like "I just don't know what to do. I have to think more about what I should do. Maybe if I try to do both. What do you think I should do?"

"What I think doesn't matter right now," I'd replied. "What you think does."

Patricia's high level of anxiety and her constant use of the word "should" was a red flag, so I gave her an assignment. "Patricia," I said, "for the next week, I want you to eliminate the word 'should' from your vocabulary."

After a moment of silence, Patricia asked, "Well, what should I say?" She then chuckled, realizing the word had slipped out again.

"Use the word 'want' for one week and see what happens. Ask yourself what you want instead of repeatedly asking what you should do."

When we had our next session on the phone, it was like I was speaking to a new person.

"Hi Patricia."

"Hi, Laura. I want to be in advertising!"

By asking herself Wisdom Access Questions instead of the information-seeking "What should I do?," Patricia was able to discover what she truly wanted. She had carved wisdom out of all her confusion simply by changing the questions she was asking. She was starting to unlock the life that would make her happiest.

■

IT'S MORE THAN THE WORDS

We have seen that changing a few words in a WAQ can make a world of difference in the quality of the answer you receive, but the truth is that changing the words alone is not enough. Getting good answers to access questions depends not only on what words you use but on where your underlying focus is. To get the best results, your underlying focus should be on solutions and forward motion for your life. When you play with the words, the questions change and their power to change your life multiplies. By committing to monitoring your inner motivation, however, you not only change your life, but begin to transform who you are.

When you can remain above the fray and stay focused on solutions and forward motion during the adversities of your life, you've begun to align with your blueprint. Your life can flow instead of getting stopped behind a dam of blame, criticism, problems, and anxiety. The focus of your inner motivation (intention) makes all the difference. In the reckoning there are really only two choices: Are you someone who intends to stay "stuck," or are you someone who intends to move forward? To use a Wisdom Access Question successfully, you must intend to move forward.

This reminds me of how I learned to drive in Manhattan. For a decade, I refused to drive there because of the terror that consumed me as taxis and buses cut me off. I would continually become exasperated, swearing and wondering, "What's wrong with these people?" One day, as I was complaining about my inability to drive myself into the city, my husband uttered a few simple words that rocked my driving world: "The thing to remember to drive well in Manhattan is to never stop moving forward."

Not only is this a great mantra for driving, it works for life. I'm not talking about motion for motion's sake, but about focusing your efforts on getting out of any potholes as soon as you can, even if you fall back into them later. Although such a shift in focus may require a fundamental change in you, it's the only way to ensure that when you ask WAQs, you're not just mouthing the words.

ARE YOU AN INFORMATION SEEKER OR A WISDOM SEEKER?

Let's take a look at what kinds of intentions you've been working with. The following list describes two very different kinds of motivation in asking questions. Most people are basically information seekers or wisdom seekers, although you may exhibit characteristics of both. Which type are you?

CHARACTERISTICS OF INFORMATION SEEKER	CHARACTERISTICS OF WISDOM SEEKER
Asks questions that are self-centered (What's wrong with me, the world, the situation in relation to how it affects me?)	Asks questions that are focused outward (What's right about me, the world, the situation? How does it add up to a whole?)
Digs for evidence to justify point of view	Explores as an objective observer to find truth
Is oriented toward problems	Is oriented toward solutions
Is territorial and assumes everything is scarce	Assumes ample resources are available
Hoards and controls information and knowledge	Sees information and knowledge as things to be shared
Reacts without thinking to problems and people	Thinks and reflects before taking action

| Must have or give answers as part of identity | Is comfortable with waiting for answers and with appearing to "not know" temporarily |
| Holds knowledge as a source of power, something to manipulate and control | Holds knowledge as a source of power, something to inspire and transform |

Each list will give you choices as to how you can use questions and help you determine which characteristics you are predisposed to. There is nothing wrong with finding yourself in the information seeker list, but you will see that you could be making better choices, asking different questions and producing less stressful outcomes if you focus on becoming the wisdom seeker.

To experience your life unfolding with ease, the shift from information seeker to wisdom seeker becomes necessary. We will explore how to make the shifts in Parts Two and Three, but let's use the next exercise to learn how your motivation may need to change. Take your time here, in order to absorb how this could transform your life.

WISDOM WRITING

For this exercise, use either the computer file you have reserved or a journal. Write down all the complaints or issues you are facing in your life right now. Here's an example:

My girlfriend wants to get married, and I'm not ready. She keeps nagging me and we're both unhappy.

Then record all the frustrating and bewildering information questions that you have about these issues.

Why is this happening? Why can't she just understand that I'm not ready? How do I get her to drop the subject?

Now jot down as many WAQs as you can that are pertinent to the issue or issues.

What will make the difference in my relationship with my girlfriend?

What needs to be said that I have not said? What can help us both get our needs met?

Notice the difference between your information questions and your access questions.

The final step in this exercise is to come up with an answer to every information question and every Wisdom Access Question that you listed. Notice the difference in the answers the two kinds of questions yield. Even though I've drilled it into your head that information questions don't move you forward, take the time to write out the answers to both kinds of questions so you can see how the inner motivation to move forward makes all the difference to this process. Watch for action steps or clarity that may come from your WAQs. Expect wisdom to flow. You can even begin to take action where it is appropriate.

WRAPPING IT UP WITH THE COACH

You have begun the excavation process that will lead to unearthing the blueprint to your best life. In this chapter, we learned these tips:

- Stop asking "Why?"
- Ask WAQs.
- Use "what?" to access wisdom.
- Keep your attention on solutions and on the future.
- Watch your motivation.
- Focus on the characteristics of the wisdom seeker rather than the information seeker in yourself.

Keep these lessons handy as we continue to work. You may want to review them as you excavate your life blueprint.

CHAPTER
2

TRAIN THE BRAIN

IN THE LAST CHAPTER, YOU BEGAN TO LEARN HOW TO USE WAQs instead of merely seeking information. What you were doing was training your brain to instinctively pursue wisdom rather than taking the less productive route you've followed before. In this chapter, you'll train your brain further, in order to channel your deepest thoughts into a course that will move you forward in your life. That is what reckoning is all about.

In this next strategy, you will reckon further by disciplining yourself to use your thinking to its maximum benefit. Up to this point, you may have been unconsciously corralling your thoughts into negative assumptions about your life and how life works in general. These assumptions may be stopping you from having what you really want. Let's take a look at how those beliefs determine the actions you are willing to take. We'll examine how changing a single thought can change the action we then take, and therefore the result we get. Just as you can train the muscles in your body to work more efficiently for your overall health, so can you train your brain to serve you better. Training your brain is a strategy that can bring you closer to unearthing your blueprint so that you can find your best life.

Focusing on training the brain to change thought always reminded me of an acting technique I learned from a wonderful commercial acting teacher named Ruth Nerken. Ruth would ask her students to choose a "ruling idea" to be the subtext of any commercial script. Let's say the product being advertised was a garden hose and the commercial was about two neighbors who always compared equipment. The ruling idea would add edge and flavor to every thought, feeling, and bit of dialogue, so the class would come up with something like "keeping up with the Joneses." From that moment forward, Ruth wouldn't let us rehearse the commercial with anything but this ruling idea in mind. The result was a very clear message, one that came through in every word the actors spoke and every gesture they made.

DEFINING BELIEFS

As I work with people to help them get what they want from their lives, I find that there are unproductive ruling ideas littering many a mind. Instead of using Ruth's term, however, I call them defining beliefs since these ideas define my clients' worlds. Defining beliefs are so deeply rooted in experience and so wonderfully steeped in evidence that they color the lens through which you look at your entire life and the world itself. They permeate your thoughts, what you say and what you do.

After years of coaching others, it's become clear to me that defining beliefs are the root of all evil in terms of not getting positive results in your life. My clients always seem to have the answers and they basically know what to do, so why aren't they doing it? In almost every case, taking positive action meant overcoming a fear or examining a long-held assumption.

Fears and assumptions are both defining beliefs, thoughts that are so well integrated into your life that they feel right even though they may actually be wrong. Training the brain to give you the thought that both *feels* right and *is* right is what this strategy is all about.

Your brain contains a truckload of rational thought. But wisdom is lurking there too. Just because you think something doesn't mean it is true or that you should believe it. What deserves belief is that which fuels your imagination and your fullest self-expression. That which points you toward the best part of you, not the fearful, hung-up part.

EXPANDING BELIEFS

Because defining beliefs are fixed, or static, they can keep you frozen, inactive, or unsuccessful. They can significantly limit your potential. The good news is that as soon as you recognize a defining belief, it can be refocused to be an expanding belief, one that points to possibility like a spotlight and can launch you into a better future.

Your deeply held beliefs are what determine what you'll make of any situation. Depending on whether they are defining or expanding, you will find either possibility or a road block.

Marcy is a perfect example of someone whose thinking had prevented her from living her best life. She had a deeply held belief that was keeping her from leading the life she wanted. This defining belief was the strong fear that if she allowed her small business to grow to where she truly hoped it would, she would lose her personal freedom, and be tied forever to a never-ending chain of work-related responsibilities. Losing her freedom was something she wanted to avoid at all costs—even that of her business's profitability. Nevertheless, at the same time, Marcy was greatly disappointed that her business had not developed and thrived as she'd envisioned. Paralyzed between two polar opposites—wanting freedom and wanting her business to take off—Marcy felt beaten and unlucky. She wondered if she would ever feel successful.

When Marcy showed up at one of my seminars, her first task was to recognize that her life was less than great not because of some strange hex, but because she was unknowingly taking only enough action to protect her defining belief. "Knowing" deep down that if the business succeeded, she would be "robbed" of her personal freedom,

Marcy had been unconsciously stopping herself from being more successful. As we began to work together, she realized that success would only increase her freedom and her ability to pay for outside help if the workload became overwhelming.

Once she had this "eureka" moment, her thinking changed and she began to see positive changes. Clients started to show up as if out of thin air. She developed a conviction that she could have a flourishing business and still have a life. As her business grew, her new confidence turned out to be a well-founded one. Now, Marcy has a thriving business, but has set limits: she is able to avoid working on weekends and on weekday evenings. She has achieved her goals without losing anything. In essence, Marcy retrained her brain to move forward into the life she wanted. She turned a limitation into a possibility.

I can point to example after example where just changing a thought, as Marcy did, resulted in a shift to more positive circumstances. Upon changing their thoughts from ones that always came to the conclusion a goal was "impossible" to ones that insisted what they wanted for themselves was definitely possible, several of my clients have reported that their phones are ringing with new opportunities.

This even happened in my own life. I wanted something, but I was convinced it would take at least six months to implement. I hesitated to take the steps to even get started, until my own coach pointed out that it was within my power to switch my thoughts and believe that what I wanted could happen more quickly. I have to admit that, although as a coach myself I should have known better, my first instinct was to blow off such "nonsense." But I tried anyway and, lo and behold, within two weeks of "changing my mind," I had in hand what I had feared would take six months to accomplish. This came about, I know, just by training my brain about what was possible. Imagine what you could accomplish if you were willing to give up defining beliefs, which lead to dead ends, for expanding beliefs, which can lead you to an open road of possibilities.

DUALITY IS A CONSTANT

It is amazing is how much duality there is in life. You can argue from either side of any issue and win—if you are arguing with yourself. All you need to do is choose which side to invest in—the one that works for you or against you; the one that shuts you down and keeps you stuck, or the one that releases the wisdom to lead you to a great life. For many people, it's scary to think that we possess all the power to make that choice.

We also possess the power to defend our beliefs, even those that don't serve us well. Soon after I started coaching, I suggested to a client that his life could be fun. He looked at me as if I had insulted every last fiber of his being and fired me on the spot. Before leaving for good, he said, "I am a serious person. Life is serious." My vision for this man had been so contrary to his entire belief system that the system itself went haywire. His reaction is a great example of how we often stubbornly cling to our beliefs, despite their possible negative effect on our life.

When you've been married to a set of beliefs for a long time, it's as if those beliefs are as familiar to your brain as a riverbed you may navigate year after year on your canoeing vacation. Your familiarity with that riverbed makes travel for that particular set of beliefs easier and easier. The beliefs flow through by habit, and they flow faster and faster over time. Therefore, when it's time to train your brain to work for you, it's as if you must portage (this is what a canoeist does when moving from one navigable river to another, carrying craft and goods overland). For you, it means moving your thoughts to a more navigable belief stream, one where you will find safe passage to the life you wish to lead.

In my own life, I often felt like depression had worn a very familiar route in my brain. My mind knew that riverbed. With the slightest trigger, all my energy would flow down that familiar stream of fear and anxiety. But, by disciplining my brain and retraining it bit by bit, I learned how to portage. I learned to pick up my canoe and go to a different river. It took years to make the riverbeds of wiser choices as navigable as those riverbeds of depression, but finally they were balanced. Small events could not trigger the old feelings with the same intensity and wrath as before.

Your mental habits may not be as deeply entrenched as mine were. Still, it won't hurt to train yourself to listen to your wisdom instead of your limiting thoughts. And nothing will make a bigger difference to training your brain than taking action. Once you decide to choose a more productive thought, taking action on it will imprint it a more navigable riverbed in your mind. The positive results you obtain through action will cement in your mind that your new expanding beliefs are true.

FROM LIMITS TO POSSIBILITY: THE EVIDENCE IS UNDENIABLE

For a belief to be a defining one, it must be backed up by a tremendous amount of supporting evidence, evidence that makes it true. The evidence is your justification for having a belief, for keeping it, and for believing in its power to define and limit you. Once you know how to choose an expanding belief, your job is to find new evidence to support the desired belief so you can change the outcome.

Any belief, negative or positive, will dictate any action you will take. If, like my client Judith, you believe that having lots of money is bad, you might have amassed in your mind a stack of supporting evidence: I will be teased and ridiculed by my friends; I'll be seen as selfish; I'll be corrupted, since money is evil. Judith, who had grown up in a wealthy home, did possess all this mental evidence because these things *did* happen to her in her youth.

As an adult, however, Judith possessed the ability to seek evidence to support an expanding belief that, as she phrased it, became: "I deserve to make a lot of money." She gathered her own evidence for this as she raised her fees for her consulting services and none of her clients balked. Judith also saw that her friends never shunned her, and she didn't become an evil person. Empowered by her successful business and her expanding belief, she soon joined an Internet startup, which made her $5 million in its first year.

There is duality in any belief a person holds: a positive side and a negative side. People make the choice about which side to focus on. For instance, we all know single people who constantly complain that all women are manipulative or that all men are jerks. Since those are their beliefs, these folks will be looking for evidence to prove them right. They will likely miss any evidence to the contrary.

Seeking evidence that supports the flip side (in this example, that there is a kind, intelligent mate out there someplace) is preferable. Evidence that supports such an expanding belief will move you along faster and create a positive momentum on its own. If you've ever heard that your beliefs determine the circumstances of your life, this is why. You may recognize what is wrong in your worldview, you may even know what action you need to take to correct your problems, but until your beliefs shift from defining to expanding, you may not even realize that you are the one responsible for the lack of results in your life.

Think of looking through the lens of a camera. You can see both the foreground and the background, but before you take a picture, you have to make a choice of which to focus the lens on. The same is true for defining and expanding beliefs: both are always present, but only the one you focus on can be the more prevalent.

DEFINING AND EXPANDING BELIEFS

Defining Beliefs	Expanding Beliefs
All men/women are jerks.	There are good men/women out there.
Money causes trouble.	Money can enable me to achieve what I want.
I can't trust anyone.	I can trust myself to choose whom to trust.

People my age don't do that.	I can do that.
I have to suffer to be thin.	I can be physically fit.
Everything is so hard.	Life can be easy.
I am not good enough.	I am right where I need to be.

EXPANDING YOUR BELIEFS—
LIVING LARGE, BUT KEEPING IT REAL

How do you live large and think bigger, yet *still* make realizable day-to-day choices? As you expand your beliefs, you will probably find it necessary to give yourself frequent reality checks in order to make sure you've chosen expanding beliefs that can truly work for you.

The key to determining this is how you feel when you choose a particular belief. If you choose a belief and, instead of firing you up, it leaves you flat or feeling as if it should have a question mark after it, then you are not yet ready for that expanding belief. If you choose one that sounds like an affirmation—"I am abundant and powerful," "I am free from pain," or "I am attracting the life of my dreams"—you have probably picked something that you wish were true, but will require some action before it is close enough to your true circumstances to make you feel excited about the possibilities and have a transforming effect.

As you choose an expanding belief, you should look for yourself to be excited and maybe even a bit afraid of its impact—those feelings confirm that you've found one that is true for you. When you pick the belief, it may feel contrived, but avoid making a quick judgment. Keep in mind that one by-product of having defining beliefs is that they protect us from change, which can be terrifying. It's normal to return to a defining belief when we focus on making an expanding belief a reality. But don't run away! Stay put.

To make an expanding belief real, choose something that could be true in your life now even if it is not yet a reality. If all that is required to make it a reality is to put focus and effort toward it, you've found the expanding belief that can cause a change in the action you take. Expanding beliefs help you uncover your true desires and form them into beliefs you can create evidence for. An expanding belief is always just real enough to warrant the right evidence. Imagination certainly comes into play, but the thoughts remain grounded in reality. You might want to become a millionaire (who wouldn't?), but if doing so is really far-fetched, your belief will become a hollow wish for something outside of what is organically tethered to you at the moment.

An expanding belief is not a wish or a goal. It is a lightning rod held out in front of you to attract evidence that will cause you to change the actions you take. You don't have to give up your desire to become a millionaire, but an expanding belief needs to be rooted close to your present circumstances and resources in order to work easily and well and help you get on the path that may eventually lead you to make such a wish a possibility. Instead of forcing "I can be a millionaire," put forth "I deserve to be financially independent." You will be able to collect evidence and take action much more easily on that one.

Expanding beliefs are yours to hold. It's your job to name them and choose to put them into effect. The next exercise is a good first step.

WISDOM IN ACTION

Carry a steno pad around with you for a day. I'd like you to use this kind of pad because each page has a line down the middle. On the top line of the first page write down the heading "Defining Beliefs" on the left side; "Expanding Beliefs" on the right side.

As you go about your daily activities, keep this pad nearby and record any thoughts that are "truths" about yourself, someone else, a situation, or life in general. If it is a thought that stops you, limits you, or undermines you, jot it down in the "Defining Beliefs" column. If it is a belief that supports who you are and what you are trying to accomplish in life, then put it under "Expanding Beliefs."

At the end of the twenty-four-hour period, tally how many of each kind of belief or thought you had. Did you have more defining beliefs than expanding beliefs? Don't worry. Coming up in this chapter is an exercise designed to help you turn the ratio around.

Did you have more expanding beliefs than defining beliefs? Good! Take action and keep collecting evidence to support your quest.

You should now have a clear picture of the quality of your beliefs and the riverbeds that are your brain's natural path. If you're not happy with what you've found, you'll have all the tools you need to change the tides by the end of this chapter.

WISDOM STORY: MEET CAROL

LIVING AN EXPANDING BELIEF

Carol came to one of my workshops and sat quietly in the back row. She was tearful, meek, and clearly racked by insecurities. She kept to herself until the second morning, when she came to me and described an epiphany she'd had. After the first day of the seminar, she had realized that she was in the grips of a defining belief that she was a worthless person. She had lots of evidence of this, memories of how people had treated her and an overall negative idea of how life had worked out for her. Carol had plenty of ammunition, so much, in fact, that she would readily disbelieve or debate anyone who told her otherwise.

Her homework after day one of the seminar was to select a new expanding belief and then seek concrete evidence of it. Carol's expanding belief was that people were well-meaning and she was worth their positive attention. As she boarded the subway on her way home, a woman smiled at her for no apparent reason. Instead of interpreting the woman's gesture as an annoyance, Carol realized that she had found the first evidence that people were kind and that she deserved their kindness. She smiled back.

Furthermore, when Carol had arrived at the seminar for day two, the man sitting next to her offered her a job. He felt compelled to do so, he said, not out of pity, but because of her willingness and determination to help herself, which he had noticed in her the day before and admired.

To this day, Carol is employed by the same company and continues to thrive in her work and home life. Carol changed her life by changing one belief.

■

WISDOM WRITING

Creating Expanding Beliefs

Now it's your turn.

Go back to your list of defining and expanding beliefs (p. 29). Which of your defining beliefs were the most damaging? Transfer those onto a new section of your Wisdom Writing computer file or onto a clean page of your Wisdom Writing notebook or journal.

If you have several beliefs, do this exercise with each one separately. For each defining belief, write down all the evidence you can think of that that belief is true. (When Carol did this exercise, her belief was that she was not worth people's kindness. As evidence, she wrote down: "People are not kind to me," "I am not getting through to people I want to be hired by," and "I am not getting along well with some of my closest friends.")

Next, for each damaging defining belief, write down what price you pay to hold on to that belief. For example, Carol's price was feeling sad, isolated, and down on her luck.

Now that you understand your defining belief better, let's explore the expanding belief that is lying dormant or hidden.

Write down the result or outcome you would like for your life right now. Carol's desired outcome was to feel valued.

Next, imagine someone who is successful at creating the result or outcome you want. What evidence would tell you this person was successful? Carol wrote that someone who had achieved her desired outcome would be treated with respect, would perform well at job interviews, and would be less needy with friends.

Finally, ask yourself what belief this "imaginary" person must have held to create that outcome. The answer you come up with is the expanding belief you can now adopt. Carol's expanding belief, if you recall, was that she was worth people's positive attention. This belief allowed her to interact with people from a position of strength.

Look over what you just wrote. Does it make you feel excited and challenged? Is it within the bounds of your current life circumstances? Then, this is your new expanding belief. Now take the action or make the adjustments that your imaginary person did in order to anchor your new belief and have it work for you.

Remember Marcy, whose defining belief was limiting the possibility of her business's growth? If we imagine Marcy doing this exercise, the outcome she would have wanted would be to increase the income from her business. The evidence required would be more clients, more money, more ease in making things happen.

Marcy did the exercise in just this way, and she arrived at the expanding belief that freed her to take action: "I can have a successful business and still have the freedom to enjoy my life." Once she really believed this, she could create her business the way she wanted it to be.

CHOOSING POSSIBILITY

Robert, a composer, came to one of my seminars with the defining belief that the kind of things I did didn't work for him. His girlfriend had bought him a ticket, and Robert was clearly an unwilling participant. Imagine my surprise when he not only returned for the second day of the seminar but seemed enthusiastic about the work we were doing. "What happened?" I asked.

"Last night," Robert replied, "I went home and chose an expanding belief that these seminars can work. Then, I worked on adopting the belief that people want to hear my music." Overnight, Robert gathered enough evidence of his new beliefs by remembering all the times he'd played his music to great response that he brought several CDs of his music to the seminar. He sold out before lunch. But his story doesn't end there. Within a couple of weeks, he was asked to perform at a high-profile event featuring Deepak Chopra.

THE MOST DEFINING BELIEF OF ALL

In good conscience, I cannot skip over the belief that I come up against the most as I coach people. "I am not good enough" is the king of defining beliefs. It runs rampant in many people's lives and careers. I know I had it for a while; you may have it yourself. I bring it up here because it is so insidious that you might not even realize it's running you, because this belief tends to trigger a neediness that keeps the believer running from his true self, chasing his personality's (ego's) needs.

If you hold this defining belief, you probably have amassed plenty of evidence to support it, and enough pain as a result, that looking for evidence to the contrary is a race against the clock and yourself. You need to know that you are good enough, and you often strive to prove this through competitiveness and manipulation of yourself and others. This is no kind of life. The antidote is not to look for evidence that you are good *enough* at something or another, but rather to find evidence that you are *good* as a person.

BEATING THE "I'M NOT GOOD ENOUGH" RAP

Ned was a newly appointed manager in a fast growing company. His bosses hired me as his coach to help him step into his expanded role, since he had just been promoted from the sales team.

Ned quickly admitted to me that he felt he was carrying a great weight. He felt insecure in his new position and, in fact, threatened by a peer who seemed to be undermining his every move. To compensate, Ned began to exhibit symptoms of what I call the hero syndrome. In an effort to prove how great and worthy he was, Ned took on endless, unnecessary responsibilities. He began to be a crutch to his staff, taking over their tasks instead of empowering them with responsibility. He was biting off more than he could chew to feel worthy of their respect.

Without digging too deeply into Ned's past, it was easy to see that he was trying to fill unmet needs due to a defining belief he was holding. The belief was that overall he was not good enough. He had so much evidence that this was true, but together we slowly but surely set out to find evidence that he *was,* in fact, good. Ned had just been promoted—he must be good. He provides for his family and is a much loved husband and father—he must be good. He knows his business and cares enough to be better at it all the time— he must be good. He is an adoring brother and son—he must be good!

Just identifying that Ned's defining belief was coloring his world allowed him to gain perspective and make some different choices in his life. He could choose to treat that belief as the truth, or not.

Ned decided to build on the evidence of his goodness that we'd assembled by taking action that reflected his new expanding belief. He did this by:

- Choosing to get home earlier every day to be the kind of father he wanted to be.
- Developing better working relationships with his staff and bosses.
- Looking more sympathetically at the man he felt was his tormentor, and seeing how he was really just as scared as Ned himself was.
- Focusing on how he was good, instead of dwelling on how he was not as good as his antagonist.

Ned collected enough evidence of his expanding belief that soon he was bitten by his old defining belief only occasionally. He trained his brain to make the better choice its automatic choice—and so can you.

■

WRAPPING IT UP WITH THE COACH

Getting to where we are meant to be involves vigorous retraining of the brain. To review some things you've learned in this chapter, it's important for you to:

- Notice your well-traveled riverbeds and how deeply grooved they are.
- Identify your riverbeds as defining beliefs.
- Change your defining beliefs to expanding beliefs.
- Collect evidence to support your new expanding beliefs.
- Keep training the brain until you don't have to anymore by taking positive action.

GAIN PERSPECTIVE

HAVING THE RIGHT PERSPECTIVE IN ANY PROBLEM OR CRISIS means seeing the situation clearly, in the proper proportion to everything else going on at the same time. It can be difficult to gauge the appropriate perspective, but generally this involves realizing that the situation confronting you is neither the end of the world nor an insignificant blip in your daily life. Gaining a healthy perspective will help guide you though personal and professional issues more efficiently, without losing your cool, and without hurting yourself or others.

Still, having perspective on your life can be tough, especially when you are highly analytical about your own life. The tendency is probably to be a bit self-centered. You are working so hard on understanding yourself that you may forget that you exist in a world filled with many other people. To gain perspective and move on to have deeper wisdom guiding your life, you need to realize that life in general is not about you and your immediate world of problems. You will not arrive at the deeper wisdom that can be yours if you live in the small world of you! It doesn't mean that you have to have some lofty mission that will touch the masses, but it does mean that for you to experience your best life, you have to get out of the way. I call this "getting over yourself."

So far, we have done a lot of reckoning with our mind to be free of its inefficiencies, but in this chapter we will begin to take the focus off our introspective selves. Now we will begin to leverage what is *right* about us and our circumstances, and use this awareness to allow our wisdom to come through. With wisdom comes perspective and with perspective comes the freedom to take action that leads to your best life.

When I say "get over yourself," I mean it as the nicest slap upside the head I hope you ever get. Once you realize that what your parents did or did not give you, or what life has given or kept from you, is not a permanent condition, you can set out to change what you feel is wrong. Talk about perspective. You are who and what you are, and you get to renegotiate that with yourself every day. So get over it and get cracking!

You can start with the ideas in this chapter. We will work to show you how insignificant you are—and that that is a *good* thing. Don't get me wrong: you are extremely powerful. However, how wisely you use that power will depend greatly on how much self-importance you give yourself.

Getting over yourself is not a matter of assuming a phony humility or playing small to not be a threat to those around you. It's about realizing that there is so much more at stake in life than your own personal problems. By comparison to the magnitude of the crises going on in the world around you, your obstacles can become tame if you *want* them to be and *only* if you want them to be! Why do you think we love to hear about other people's problems so much? Why are most of us so fascinated by disaster? Because by realizing the depth of suffering that can and does exist in this world, we gain perspective. We gain a brutal understanding of just how fragile life is and how much good there is to embrace.

By absorbing how teeny most of our cares are, we gain the freedom to address them. The information that we need to give us direction and solutions to our problems is accessible once we get over our powerful self-absorption.

FEAR: WISDOM'S ENEMY

Whenever I ask my clients and workshop participants what keeps them from doing what they all seem to know they need to do, the answer is always, unequivocally, fear. Fear—whether in the form of high emotion, anger, or dramatic outpourings of panic—is the greatest enemy to your own wisdom. Wisdom is blocked because of fear's intensity. Fear is the most insidious and powerfully negative tool the mind has. Even worse, fear has the capacity to disguise itself as good judgment.

The bad news is that no matter how hard you try to conquer your fears, they will never go away completely. So your work in this chapter is not to eliminate fear, but to dramatically improve your relationship with it. The first step is to realize that, however much your fear grips you, you have an equal amount of greatness in you. Our fear is directly proportional to our greatness. If you are a fearful person, you probably don't have all that you want and do have a tendency to devote more time to your fear than your greatness. Like hanging out with the "wrong crowd," it is having a bad influence on you. To improve your relationship with fear necessitates that you get better at knowing when you are experiencing a negative reaction to your circumstances that it's due to fear, and not necessarily reality. Second, it takes knowing what your choices are and, third, getting a handle on how to disengage fear's grip on your mind so that wisdom can flow.

Gaining perspective is the most significant way to begin to reckon with your fear. Let's look at some ways to help you gain perspective on fear so you can move more freely toward your life blueprint.

YOU CAN'T TAKE THINGS PERSONALLY

When we experience a less than positive exchange with someone or a negative situation in our life, we tend to immerse ourselves in the experience. We often find it hard to put the conversation in the past or look at what happened with an objective eye. Instead, we take the exchange very personally. How could we not? It happened to us, right? Yes, but I'm sure you know people—maybe even you your-self—who are still suffering over something that happened to them or that someone did to them weeks, months, or even years ago. We often find ourselves unable to move on to a solution because we can't get over what happened. To gain perspective when something bad happens, it is necessary to detach from it, to make the effort to ob-serve the situation objectively. It's natural to feel disappointed, we must move out of it by separating it from ourselves.

In order to step outside of an event and observe it, you need to increase your self-awareness so that you can catch yourself before you get swept up in and obsessed by the drama of what's going on. This means, for instance, stopping yourself before you react to a per-sonal attack or an unwanted circumstance. A tall order indeed—but if you can separate, you'll be able to avoid letting the situation get the best of you. You'll be able to form an appropriate response, one that allows you to stretch and become the mature person you want to be in the situation instead of a person who reacts unthinkingly, from primal instinct. The minute you enter the "danger zone" with some-one and you feel a strong reaction coming on, you need to develop a shield to deflect the bad attitude or harmful words coming at you. You don't want the situation at hand to push your buttons, so the im-portant thing to do is to get this person out of your space gracefully and without contempt.

The secret to being able to develop that shield and not react neg-atively is to realize that people come from the limit of their own growth and experience. When you accept that their attack on you is really about them and not you, perhaps you can forgive them and move on. Granted, this may be easier said than done, but when you do it, you maintain the freedom to keep your life moving forward, toward your best life.

Even when you face a tragic circumstance—the loss of a job or a loved one, or the diagnosis of a severe illness—it is not personal. You were not branded for hard time. Feel the pain, experience the disap-pointment, but try to shift yourself to a mind-set of learning all you can from the situation, instead of surrendering to victimhood. This is the only way forward. No one wants these things to happen, but even major disappointments hold the potential to turn our heads in the direction of the blueprint for our best life.

NOT TAKING IT PERSONALLY

Remember Ned, our young manager from the last chapter? I mentioned he had a nemesis at work, someone who just drove him crazy. Ned complained to me that this colleague was undermining him, rushing to be the first one to share ideas with management so Ned would look ineffective by comparison.

Ned was interpreting this man's actions in a way that made them very personal, as if the coworker was acting not out of his own self-interest, but out of a desire to hurt Ned. But when Ned and I looked at his problem together, we discovered that certain of his buttons kept getting pushed. His own insecurities and feelings of not being good enough (that defining belief and a very real fear) came up every time. Ned finally realized that his foe was not doing anything to him, but rather he was doing it to himself. Once he saw this, Ned was able to "unhook" by not taking it personally. He could avoid letting his emotions get the best of him. Ned even noticed that there were things he could learn from his "foe," who both possessed a level of confidence Ned wanted to emulate and yet was the kind of manager Ned did *not* want to be. In fact, instead of feeling in competition with this man, Ned began to recognize his own unique strengths, many of which were quite different from those of his colleague. Ned stopped trying to match his colleague as the "idea man," and focused instead on becoming a facilitator for his peers. He began to sit back at meetings instead of looking for the place to jump in with a brilliant new concept. Instead, he was brilliant at helping people hear one another, and he was a master at encouraging his staff to express their ideas clearly. Ned became the kind of manager and leader he wanted to be.

Ned's ability to not take his colleague's actions personally freed him to use his natural talents and be more useful to his company. Ned got over himself and his brilliance and wisdom were able to shine through.

■

Not taking things personally is a lesson I learned vividly in my own life when I was still struggling to make it as an actor in New York City. I frequently had to walk along the crowded lunchtime sidewalks of Fifth Avenue. The sidewalks were a sea of bodies that seemed to stretch for miles in front of me. I could barely see where I was going and I often feared that if I didn't keep the pace, I'd be trampled. Most of the time I found this annoying, swearing under my breath whenever a stray package happened to brush against me or another pedestrian's elbow grazed me. Every person who got in my way was to be punished by the intensity of my gaze and the thoughts that followed. It seemed that the more I resented this experience, the more often I had it.

But one sunny spring day I suddenly noticed that no one was bumping into me on the street. It was as if the sea of people parted to let me through. I thought back to all the times that I'd been hit by briefcases and umbrellas and felt pummeled and aggravated walking on the very same street. What was different? I was. The day alone had put me into a happy mood and I felt as if I was emanating a positive energy that glowed at least three feet ahead of me.

The times I had to fight my way through the crowds were the times I was feeling just as angry as everyone else around me seemed to be. But the sea parted for me when I was able not to care what those around me did. I had not made their actions personal to me, and, as a result, I experienced ease and flow among the chaos.

WISDOM IN ACTION

Write down the names of people whom you still hold grudges against or feel less than peaceful about. (If you don't have any, good for you, but be sure you're being honest.) Explore what you took personally in each situation. Did an old friend neglect you? Your parents upset you? A neighbor disrespect you? If you were to unhook yourself from the emotion and relive the relationship again, what might you do differently? What would you say if you ran into this person now? What could you do to no longer care about what transpired? Write down specific actions you could take to be sure these scenarios never come back to bite you again.

TOUCH ANOTHER LIFE TO FIND YOURS

One of the women attending a recent London seminar of mine approached me afterward and told me she was very well-known and had been involved in a very public scandal. I didn't recognize her and she didn't tell me her name or provide any further details. In the aftermath of the scandal, she had been trying to make herself feel better by spending lots of money on shopping and vacations. But now she wanted some concrete advice about getting her life back on track.

My suggestion was simple: "Get your hands dirty! Go out and hold dying babies or sing to an old person or serve food in a homeless shelter," I said. "You'll find yourself again." She seemed stunned for a moment but then something seemed to register with her. She thanked me and left.

The advice I gave this woman basically boils down to this: nothing will pull you out of your own stuff faster than realizing your stuff isn't so bad. Intellectually, you know that many other people are worse off than you, but seeing what really is going on in the world firsthand is a wonderful way to put your own life in perspective. You and your problems are not as important as you think they are. Nothing will make you realize this more clearly—or make you feel better about yourself—than when there are grateful eyes looking back at you because you improved someone else's condition a little bit.

"That's all well and good," you might respond, "but will it make my problems go away? Will it pay my mortgage? Will it heal my child's life-threatening illness?" Maybe not. But it will give you per-spective. A mountain climber can't get a sense of where she is on the mountain by staring at the ground beneath her feet; she must look up or down to get a sense of where she must go next. Similarly, through gaining perspective, you may gain the clarity to hear your own wisdom directing you to take a certain action or find a resource that can help get you where you want to go.

WISDOM IN ACTION

I call this the self-centered challenge. For an entire week, I want you to strike the word "I" from your vocabulary. This is the most overused word in the English language, and you'll find it's not easy to avoid. As you realize how much you use "I," you'll find yourself much more interested in other people. This exer-cise may make you feel baffled, humbled, or even a little sad. Such feelings aren't permanent. They're just the result of your ego's shrinking and feeling very sorry for itself. Having a healthy ego is not a bad thing, but we could all stand to gain a little per-spective on our place in the world. This perspective invites the ease and satisfaction I've been promising.

GOING TOO FAR

Although helping others is a very effective tool in helping you gain perspective on your life, it's also important that you not go too far. If helping someone else results in your neglecting your own life, then it defeats the purpose of gaining a healthy perspective. Being of ser-vice to people should not mean sacrificing yourself. When you sacri-fice in this way, you end up not getting over yourself but losing yourself.

Giving has nothing to do with loss. Giving need only be sharing, and when you share, you lose nothing. However, if you are avoiding your own pain or responsibilities in taking care of others, not only do you not gain perspective but the help you are giving may actually be less effective than it would be if you were clearly giving to share.

This is because when we overwhelm ourselves with helping other people, we often become resentful, stressed, overburdened, and even numb. But when we give to others in a balanced way, we *find* ourselves instead of losing ourselves in the process.

GETTING SOME DISTANCE

Besides doing for others and not taking things personally, great perspective can come from simply getting some distance from a situation. This can be done literally: If you are having trouble at work, get up and go outside for a walk to take yourself out of the environment that's causing you so much stress. Even if you are in the middle of something, break your thinking pattern by clearing your head with a walk and you'll be so much more productive when you get back.

Getting distance can also be metaphorical. Sometimes we need mental space more than physical space. If you are having trouble with a relationship, try moving your mind away from it by engaging your creativity. Draw a picture about how you feel, do some work on a workshop or craft project, read a short story or even a kid's book. All these activities take you someplace else mentally and are sometimes enough to gain the perspective you need to come back to the relationship and deal with the issues more objectively.

If literal and metaphorical distance do not release the grip your mind has on you, I'm afraid you'll have no other choice than to give up and laugh.

FIND THE LEVITY

"Oh, come on, lighten up." Don't you just love hearing that when you feel like you have a justifiable reason for not being happy? Yet by suggesting that perhaps you need to chill out or adjust your attitude, these people may not realize just how very astute and wise they are being in their request.

Wisdom alone cannot get through when your thoughts are dense or heavy. Laughter lightens the mind's load and relieves the tension that keeps your heavy thoughts circling around and around.

Laughter can free your thoughts from their tendency to go down a negative riverbed. Laughter distracts you from what's bothering you, giving you a sense of detachment that allows your intuition to kick in. As a result, it enables your mind to make room for unusual solutions to problems as well as for wisdom to come through. It allows you to get in touch with the part of you that is wiser and might be more rational than your emotional self. Laughter dulls the edge of the knife your inner critic wields. Since it can do all these things, is it any wonder that we are grateful for comic relief during a serious movie or play or even an intense business meeting?

Stephen is a wonderful example of someone who just needed to laugh. He sat in the front row at one of my seminars and seemed riveted by what I had to say. When I asked for a volunteer to come up onstage, he stood up and asked for my help. He wanted to have more fun in his life, he declared.

With all due respect, Stephen was far from dour, but he looked as if he hadn't even cracked a smile in many years. Intuitively, I knew that if he was to have any chance at having more fun, he needed to have a reference point for it immediately. So I began to laugh and asked him to join me. It wasn't easy for him, so I asked the audience to join us. Soon, the whole place was in tears as we laughed until our sides ached. Finally, I saw a real laugh emerge from Stephen. When it did, his skin practically changed color. He was benefiting from increased oxygen and his face changed to pink from ashen. He experienced fun, even if only for a moment. He turned to leave the stage with a demure "Thank you," and then suddenly turned back, gave me a huge hug, and shouted as if surprised at himself: "I can have fun!"

WISDOM IN ACTION

Find a humor mentor, someone whose sense of humor you delight in. Study this person, what he finds funny, where his humorous outlook on life comes from. If you are already a fun lover, stretch by enjoying the masters. Get a video or an audio recording of a professional comedian who appeals to you. Watch and listen for how she looks at life to find its humor. You can even take a stand-up comedy class! Think of it as training for your mind.

Just as there are times when helping others crosses the line, we need to be careful with laughter as a way of gaining perspective. That's because it can sometimes serve to hide feelings. And it's common for people to deflect intimate, deep emotions with humor to avoid feeling vulnerable. I once attended a wedding where the bride cracked jokes and mugged to the attendees during the ceremony because she was terribly uncomfortable with the profound sanctity of the moment.

Humor is also used as a way of expressing an opinion without being genuine. I'm sure you can think of many times in your life when someone cracked a joke at your expense, only to take it back, upon seeing your reaction, with an indignant "Just kidding." In fact, the person being kidded was not you but the joker, who convinced himself that you would not notice or feel the true intention behind his humor. When humor is used to avoid telling the truth, it loses its ability to clear your brain and allow your inner wisdom to emerge. When humor is truthful, it can be just as powerful in its impact as a profound philosophical insight. Just as a profound insight can illuminate a new possibility, so can humor provide a way to look at something in a whole new way.

Hiding Behind the Joke

Bruce was a well-liked businessman who was known in his community for his sense of humor. I was hired to coach some of his key people, and in the process, I became his coach as well. Through talking to him firsthand and hearing about his behavior from his employees, I quickly learned that he tended to use humor as a weapon instead of addressing people's problems in a more honest way. He'd say, "If you'd gone to a good school, you'd have been able to figure this out," or, "Keep dressing like that and we'll be attracting every pervert in the county." Not very nice—or effective.

When I pointed out to Bruce that he seemed unable to communicate what he really felt in an appropriate way, he reacted defensively. But after a few weeks, he finally admitted that he knew he was sometimes hard on people and thought that using humor was a way to soften his blows. He saw this was a cop-out, allowing him to not take responsibility for what he was saying—because, after all, it was just a joke.

Together, Bruce and I worked on ways in which he could communicate more honestly. Every time he was about to make a wisecrack, he made an effort to stop himself and ask first, "What am I *not* communicating here?" He could then address the real issue. For example, instead of the wisecracks he wielded above, he could say things like: "We're all under a lot of pressure, but let's do our best to find a solution to this problem," or "I'm concerned that your attire doesn't reflect the kind of respect for your position that will encourage others to respect your work."

Over the course of a few months, Bruce began to see a dramatic increase in sales among his associates. They freely admitted feeling more energized and motivated about their work once Bruce's acerbic humor stopped and honest feedback and conversations began.

The bottom line is that humor and laughter can transform us and those around us in a positive way—as long as they are not being used to hurt, or to gain or wield power.

GAINING PERSPECTIVE BY CHOOSING TO LOVE

Another tool that we can draw upon to shift our perspective is love. We've all heard the merits of loving ourselves, loving others, and loving the planet, right? But not all of us have been able to use all that love to positively affect the daily transactions of our lives. The pace of our lives and the intensity of our emotions or personality often prevent us from acting with love as a code. It may be hard to be kind to ourselves or others, or to face a critical situation with the perspective love can provide. But in order to think of love as a fundamental code, one by which we can live, it may help to compare it with another code, one by which many of us are already guiding our life: power.

In the time we live in, power is still defined very much by external references, such as money, status, position, or the ability to influence others. We are powerful if we have these things, and powerless if we don't. They can be taken away.

Love cannot be taken away. You can always choose to love someone, something, or a situation, whether you feel those things merit your love or not. That is true power. Love, as a choice, is power. Instead of choosing to hate, fight, undermine, or manipulate, you could choose to love, and that choice might help you find a more positive solution to any problem. For example, if someone betrayed my friendship, I could decide to banish that person from my life and forever speak of how he did me wrong. On the other hand, I could gain a quick exit to the pain by choosing love to find perspective. I don't have to agree with what the person did, nor do I have to forgive him. I just have to choose to love myself and him and elevate myself to the place where I can see he did me a favor. Now I know he was not as true a friend as I thought, and I can go on in my life with a lesson learned. A much more powerful choice, I think, than holding on to bitterness, even though many would feel I was justified to do so.

When it comes to love, we often don't honor ourselves *enough* and therefore have little or no wisdom-producing perspective. Loving yourself or someone else does not mean abandoning self by overindulging in the feeling or its intoxicating effects. It doesn't mean sacrificing yourself to love someone or even merely to have another person like you. It means harnessing your emotion and awareness to create the most good in your life. That means that if a relationship is destructive, you should get out. It's not an invitation to love harder. There is no power in loving harder—only in loving better.

FINDING PERSPECTIVE BY CHANGING THE DEFINITION OF LOVE

Maureen was a smart woman in her early thirties who came to me to do some career and life planning. She was engaged to an older man who had children from a previous marriage and did not want any more. Maureen worked for a large bank but longed to own her own business someday. We had come up with a plan to improve her satisfaction with her current job, which included asking for a raise and revamping her responsibilities.

Naturally, as we discussed her career, Maureen's impending wedding kept coming into the conversation. I had a strong sense that this marriage was a mistake. As we explored her job, her desired new business, and her upcoming marriage, it was clear to me that Maureen's definition of love was erring on the side of self-sacrifice. She was struggling with the realization that by marrying this man she was giving up the chance to have children of her own. It wasn't appropriate for me to tell Maureen what to do, but I did tell her how I felt: "What I want for you, Maureen, is a relationship where you don't have to twist yourself into a pretzel in order to fit in." She seemed hardly to acknowledge my comment, but two weeks later she reported that she had ended her engagement. She was quitting her job and taking a long trip abroad in order to explore herself and her life.

Until then, Maureen's definition of love was to do what everyone else wanted her to, and to love harder meant giving up more of herself to make it work. When she learned to love better and therefore learned to love herself, her perspective changed. She saw that choosing to love herself meant that she had to reclaim the pieces of herself she had compromised. Once she made the switch, the direction she needed to take was clearer and the action she took immediate. Wisdom had replaced anxiety and confusion. She had gained the perspective that gave her the clarity to do the right thing for herself.

RECLAIMING POWER AS A WAY TO LOVE OURSELVES

Most people think that loving ourselves means accepting ourselves for who we are, shortcomings and all, and being nice to ourselves with gifts and nurturing gestures. That's part of it. But the greatest love of self is keeping an eye on where we distribute our power.

Earlier I said that choosing to love, even in adverse situations, was a way to gain perspective and define true power. Now I take that one step further to say that watching where you distribute that power reflects on how well you love yourself. Do you choose to love out of fear in order protect yourself from a consequence, or do you love out of believing in the better part of yourself and other people? When you choose to love from fear, you are not loving yourself, you are doing what you think you have to in order to get what you want. When you respect yourself and therefore love yourself, you will get what you want and with more ease and satisfaction. You will not be compromising yourself.

As a coach, I spend a lot of time helping people reclaim power. They do this not by usurping it from a friend or boss, but by reclaiming pieces of themselves they have given away when they really do not want to, whether in a relationship, a business deal, a meeting, or another detail of their life.

The place to begin amassing power is within yourself. Look at where you are giving it away. Look for the places where it is leaking out of you like air from a punctured tire. It is usually not hard to locate: it is where you are abandoning yourself, where action must now be taken. Getting that power back and keeping it where it should be is what it is to love yourself.

WISDOM STORY: MEET DIANNE

RECLAIMING POWER

Dianne, a homemaker, came to me because she wanted to become more assertive in communicating with her husband and friends. In listening to her speak, it was soon clear to me that she needed to recognize how often she gave away power by unnecessarily apologizing for herself. On the telephone, she would start a conversation by saying, "I'm sorry, is Linda there?" She was telegraphing that she had weak boundaries and could be counted on to overextend herself to please others.

Once I pointed it out to her, Dianne watched herself very closely. She listened for how often she apologized for herself. At the grocery store, she would ask a clerk, "If you have a moment, could you possibly stop to help me with this purchase?" At the bank she would say to the teller, "I don't mean to bother you, but when could you be free to talk with me?" And when a friend reached for a napkin in her kitchen, she'd rush to help and say, "Oh, I'm sorry. I should have done that for you."

She had never been conscious of how often she betrayed herself with her words. Discovering how often she put the needs of others first in her speech changed Dianne's world. She removed "apology language" from her vocabulary. She soon began to stand up straighter, speak louder, and articulate what she wanted more quickly.

In just a few months, the people in Dianne's life were acknowledging how she had changed. Her newfound self-confidence allowed her to reclaim power in her marriage by no longer being afraid of conflict and by addressing matters head-on with her husband. It also allowed her to negotiate part ownership of a documentary film to which she had previously given a great deal of time without asking for anything in return. Overall, she felt the quality of almost all her relationships was higher and more pleasurable. She no longer felt like everyone's doormat, with no tools to help herself. Reclaiming her power required first that she improve her relationship with herself, which in turn transformed her relationships with others.

WISDOM IN ACTION

It's time for action. I challenge you in the next week to increase the power you have by taking it back from where it does not belong. Examine the recent past, looking for situations in which you have compromised yourself. Record in your journal or computer what these situations were, and be specific about what happened and who was involved. If you were disappointed by a friend who did not keep a promise, for example, and you were afraid to ask about it, write: "Don said he would visit this weekend and then did not show up or phone to say he wasn't coming. I didn't call him on it, although it's the second time he's done something like this."

In every situation you've written about, think about what you can do to reverse the loss of power. Your perspective will be changed as you see your power increase and as you realize that the key to moving your life forward in a positive way has roots in this kind of self-love.

EXPLORING GRATITUDE AS A BLUEPRINT ACCELERATOR

One more way of gaining a healthy perspective on your life is through expressing gratitude. Showing that you are grateful for what you have multiplies your ability to attract what you think you lack. If you choose to validate what you lack by harping on it, you are draining yourself of the energy you need to focus on what you have that can be leveraged to your great benefit. As your coach, I am always looking for what's right about you to help you build your future. Recognizing how much you already have and being grateful for it is key to accomplishing that future.

Taking stock of what's working lessens the leaden effect of focusing on what is missing. It turns up the volume on possibility. Finding out what you're grateful for allows you to move forward more quickly. I can't tell you how many people have approached me, bitter about their jobs or life circumstances, only to hear me ask: "What can you be grateful for?" They look at me quizzically, but I continue: "What have you learned from your unsatisfying experience? Did you learn a new skill? Have you discovered what tasks or circumstances no longer suit you? Great! Now what do you have to do?"

WISDOM STORY: MEET RICK

GRATITUDE'S TRANSFORMING EFFECT

Things had not been going Rick's way. He hated where he lived, he resented his wife's inability to snap out of a funk, and he was not satisfied with his career. There wasn't a whole lot in his life that he felt grateful for. Although Rick was struggling to overcome all these circumstances, nothing he did seemed to break him of his frustrations and dissatisfaction.

It was time for Rick to get over himself and gain a new perspective on his life. Rick took stock of his material possessions, his work experience, and his marriage. In all three categories, he had much to boast of. Rick saw that his current work had given him the experience he needed to pursue a dream position he'd recently heard about in New York City. He saw that he had much to appreciate about his wife and that he had learned a lot about himself by being in his relationship with her. While this helped bring them closer together, it also ultimately led them to the decision that separating would be the best step for both of them. As Rick was searching for something to be grateful for about the small town where he lived, he realized that at the least it had convinced him that he belonged in a cosmopolitan city.

Up to this point, Rick had been feeling victimized; gratitude had been the last thing on his mind. But, once he changed his focus from the negative in his life to the positive, he gained a new perspective and was able to see clearly what he needed to do next.

Rick had been in pain, but instead of taking his anger, frustration, and disappointment out on others, or inflicting punishment on himself, he turned inward and was able to set himself free by multiplying what was good about his life. Rick ended up moving to Manhattan, where he accepted that dream job. His life opened up, and he felt more alive than he had in years.

WISDOM WRITING

Taking stock of what you can be grateful for on a daily basis becomes an important way to make this way of gaining perspective a habit. Try it now by writing down ten things you can be grateful for today. These could be your health, your family, the roof over your head, your job, your money, your new car, your neighbor, your friends, and so on. It could also be more circumstance-oriented—a particularly good conversation with a coworker, for instance, or a chance meeting with a long-lost friend, or the fact that a woman on the grocery line gave you her place so you could check out sooner.

Now go back to the complaints about your life that you listed in chapter 1. Look at them with new eyes and try to find something to be grateful for about the items that are problems now. What have you learned from having these problems—how are they stretching you and forcing you to grow? As annoying as they may be, examining them through the lens of gratitude may uncover the hidden positives about them.

As a third part to this writing, jot down how your perspective has shifted because of this exercise. What might you do differently? Is there any action you would like to take now because of it? Write down the changes you'd like to make.

WRAPPING IT UP WITH THE COACH

Gaining perspective is the third and final strategy of the Reckoning stage. A healthy perspective on your life will help put you on track to where you are meant to be. Working to maintain the right perspective is a lifelong investment, and you've learned a variety of techniques that will enable you to do that. Even when things are going well for you, remember to:

- Avoid taking things personally.
- Let go of old grudges.
- Help other people.
- Say "I" less.
- Look for levity.
- Choose to love.
- Reclaim your power by loving yourself.
- Focus on what you have to be grateful for instead of what you lack.

PART TWO

THE DOING

MASTERING YOUR PHYSICAL WORLD BY "DOING"—THAT is, by putting your wisdom into action—is the key to unlocking the magic of your best life.

In this section we will address two aspects of your physical world: your physical body and the life circumstances around you. First, I'll show you how to observe yourself and your surroundings with more care, and then we'll work on searching your innate wisdom for the actions that can truly make a difference in finding what you want. This will allow you to get off the "trying to have it all" treadmill that most of us live on. This part of the book will show you what keeps you in overdrive and how to get out. Taking action is key. Recognizing the right action to take is mastery.

I find that many people chase success, hoping it will somehow fill the void they have not been able to fill in their lives. They don't realize that if they were to stop and find ways to become responsible for their present circumstances, they could then begin to master their lives. The future they crave will then have a safe landing strip. Chasing the future keeps what you want at bay. Accepting responsibility for the present invites your extraordinary future to come find you.

The physical world is your testing ground. It tests your mettle, your survival skills, your smarts, and everything in between. Most of us assume that the test is to "make it"—to succeed, to make our parents proud, to make something of ourselves. If only we knew that acing the test requires simply that we do everything in our power to make our life work. This does not necessarily mean you will be granted an idyllic life. Making your life work does not guarantee you'll have everything you want, but it will mean that the struggle has been reduced and that fulfillment has returned. It requires becoming attuned to what must stay and what must go in your life at any given moment and being honest about what you really want instead of settling only for what you think you can have. As a result, you will feel like you are creating your life by your own choices, not from a list of obligations and expectations you feel trapped by.

In order to make this happen, we will examine your life closely to determine where you should spend your time and energy to get the most from your life. You will learn to discern the clues your body can give you about living your best life. After that, you'll make a simple contract to underscore with action all the emotional Reckoning you did in Part One. From there, you'll discover that you come equipped with a "lucrative purpose"—something you are meant to be doing in life that will satisfy you physically, spiritually, and financially. Finally you will learn how to magnetize yourself—attracting positive outcomes to yourself and repelling negative ones by allowing your innate wisdom to guide your physical action. One might say this is the beginning of the fun part.

ACT ON WHAT YOU FEEL, NOT ON WHAT YOU THINK

U P UNTIL NOW, WE HAVE FOCUSED ON WHAT YOU ARE THINK-ing rather than on what you are doing in your life. After all, your thoughts determine the actions you'll be willing to take. But you can't just think yourself to that point. Here we will start to integrate your mind with your body. We are going to raise your awareness of your body in order to determine the actual actions that will get you to live your best life.

Beyond thinking, to experience wisdom you have to *feel* and to know what you are feeling. We can all recognize feelings like anger, frustration, sadness, elation, and love—extreme emotions that are easy to identify. Yet, the clues to our best lives do not lie in the extremes, but rather in our more subtle feelings, such as sensing the difference between passion and adrenaline or between inspiration and ego.

To recognize subtle feelings, we need to be sensitively attuned. We must be in a state of calm to fully feel them. Too often we are just simply too busy, exhausted, overwhelmed, anxious, or revved up to find that necessary calm. We become desensitized to the subtleties of feeling by adrenaline, busyness, distractions, dramas, and the self-centeredness of chasing what we want. We become numb to our emotions because we get into the habit of avoiding feelings that make us uncomfortable or that demand we take time to deal with them.

Doing as much as we do in our busy worlds, on a daily basis, causes most of us to rev our bodies into overdrive, running on adrenaline in order to have the energy to meet our demands. Running on adrenaline stresses our bodies. It's something we're equipped to do for only short periods of time. But we often are in overdrive for longer periods, which eventually wears down our systems. Too much stress can result in physical or emotional exhaustion, mood swings, insomnia, and even illness and disease.

Our work in this chapter is to get you off the busy treadmill of your life by getting you in touch with what you really feel and want on a visceral level. I will help you learn to admit your feelings, to feel them deeply, and to be so sensitive to them that you are never so busy in your daily life that you ignore them. You will begin to feel your way to the awareness required to be in partnership with your body and your life, rather than being run by them. Once you recognize your feelings, you will begin to trust them to guide you to actions that can affect your life positively and immediately.

ARE YOU HEARING WHAT YOUR SUBTLE FEELINGS HAVE TO SAY?

Your body holds the clues to the blueprint of your best life. Let's take a look at what may be in the way of your feeling the subtleties of your own wisdom as it is expressed in your own body.

Place a checkmark on the line next to each statement below that you would say is true about you.

_____ I work more than forty hours a week.

_____ I live on the edge financially.

_____ I exercise fewer than three times per week.

_____ I have great conflict in some work relationships.

_____ I drink more than one caffeinated beverage per day.

_____ I'd like more quality time with my family.

_____ I need more space in my home.

_____ Emotional issues often get in my way.

_____ I have outstanding bills and paperwork.

_____ People always depend on me in a pinch.

_____ I abuse alcohol and/or drugs.

_____ I have strained personal relationships.

_____ My work environment impedes productivity.

_____ I engage in a fun activity fewer than two times a week.

_____ I wish for more satisfying work.

_____ I have more than my share of problems.

_____ I overpromise my time and what I can accomplish.

_____ I am self-conscious about my appearance.

Give yourself 1 point for each checkmark. Tally your score and analyze the results with the guidelines below.

1–2: Congratulations! You are probably in touch with most of what challenges you, and you can see where the blemishes are. Now is the time to take action on them so you are free to follow your own wisdom.

3–6: You've started to enter the "unconscious zone," where you are becoming resigned to the circumstances in your life. It's not an ideal state for hearing your own wisdom and being connected to what you feel.

7–10: Life must feel terribly overwhelming to you. You're not in a place where wisdom can be heard. Radical action will be required.

11 or more: You are completely in reactive mode, barely keeping your head above water. It would be almost impossible to hear yourself think, much less decipher how you feel and what you really want.

The things mentioned in the above quiz are distractions. They take up a lot of time and energy, and yet they're exactly what keep you from feeling that you have what you want. They point you away from yourself, not toward yourself. What you truly desire may be getting sacrificed to the demands of your daily life.

Things don't have to be this way. Our work in "The Doing" will help you expand your scope of what is possible, so your life can revolve around what matters to you most.

In order to connect with your body and its emotions to find your wisdom's clues, let's first evaluate how far your daily activities have taken you away from what you say truly matters to you.

HOW FAR ARE YOU FROM WHAT YOU SAY YOU WANT?

On a blank piece of paper, write down the things you most want for your life, in order of importance. This could be health and well-being, family, romantic relationships, friends, leisure, hobbies, well-paying work, spiritual life, religious life, community service, creative pursuits, adventure, education, etc. It's been shown that we can do only three to five things at a time if we are to do them well. So your next step is to choose five items from your list and put them in order of priority. The item you would want if you could be granted only one thing in life should be written down first. Item 2 is what would be important if you could have just one more thing. Continue until your list has a maximum of five items.

Here's an example of what one list might look like at this point:

1. Health and well-being
2. Family
3. Satisfying, well-paying work
4. Friends
5. Community service

To the right of each item jot down the order in which those things appear in your life now. For example, if I say health and well-being is the number-one priority in my life, but I haven't exercised regularly in six months, it might really merit a score of five. And if I don't do anything to improve or maintain my health at all in my real life, then I'll put a zero in that column. (You may have a few zeros, but don't worry—you're not alone. Every audience I have ever shared this with has a predominance of zeros in the lineup.)

The finished version of the list above would be something like:

1. Health and well-being   5
2. Family   2
3. Satisfying, well-paying work   1
4. Friends   0
5. Community service   0

Our hypothetical coachee says his health is important, but he does almost nothing about it. He wants to have friends and feel connected to the community, but he does even less in those areas.

If you see a lot of zeroes on your list, my mean little trick has succeeded. In having you take this quiz, I wanted to wake you up to the fact that *you are not spending your time doing what you say is important to you*. You are probably spending your time trying to accomplish all that you think has to come before you are allowed to reward yourself by attending to your own desires. No, no, no! Living this way desensitizes you to what you really want. This, in turn, is leading you further and further away from your goal—the life you want to be living.

FEELING YOUR PRIORITIES

By now you've assessed what kinds of things may keep you living a "treadmill existence," and you've got a clearer picture of what keeps you from having time for the things that matter to you most. In my experience as a coach, when people are pulled in several directions this way, it is hard to create significant forward motion, goal attainment, and satisfaction in life. The antidote is to get back in touch with what you truly want and get back to feeling again.

When you make contact with your feelings, you can sense when you have betrayed yourself by taking on yet another obligation that distances you from your goals and priorities. Obviously, obligations like showing up at your job in the morning can't be avoided, but when you get back in touch with what you feel, you may have to admit that even the job could warrant some changing. Obligations become "shoulds" in your life—the things you think you *must* do and over which you think you have no power. It is the "shoulds" that keep you away from what is important to you. Here's what you do:

- Memorize your list of priorities.
- Use the memorized list as a measuring stick against every demand on your time.
- Arrive at the point where you can sense your true priorities in your cells. Eventually, you will not let anything come between you and what truly matters.

You can change the list in the preceding exercise over time, but always keep it at five items. It's critical to *feel* the difference between a true desire and everything else that vies for your attention. And it is critical that you trust this feeling.

WHAT YOU THINK YOU CAN HAVE VERSUS WHAT YOU WANT

So many times we ignore what we want (what we feel) in the name of what we think we can have. We are so fast to doubt or complicate what we truly desire with excuses, preconceived notions of what's possible, and defining beliefs before we have even tried to make our desire come to fruition. The worst part is we don't even know we are doing it. We hear the wisdom of the desire, but we immediately dismiss it in favor of what we think we can have.

For example, during one of my "wisdom workshop teleclasses,"

Lewis, a salesman, asked me to coach him on how he could increase his numbers. When I asked him how many sales he wanted and how he could go about getting them, he never seemed emotionally connected to this goal. So I asked him what it was he really wanted. He repeated a dollar amount and how many sales that would require. But his voice was again flat and there was no excitement behind it.

"No," I said, "if you were really honest, and I could wave my magic coaching wand and you could have it right now, what would you want?"

Lewis thought for a minute, then his voice lit up. "My own business." The minute he said this, Lewis realized he had been settling for what he thought he could have instead of what he truly wanted. He really wanted his own business, but he was settling for more sales at his current job. The next time I heard from him, just a few weeks later, Lewis had left his job and was pursuing his dream of becoming an entrepreneur.

Most of us do what Lewis was doing. We ignore what we truly want, thinking we can't possibly have it, and then proceed to get frustrated with the lack of results we see or the lack of motivation we experience as we try to accomplish the goal we set in consolation. Life gives us what we expect it to give us. In other words, we get what we expect.

Breaking through to bigger possibilities isn't about positive thinking, nor is it reserved for the privileged. Breakthroughs occur when you respect the wisdom you are wired for. Getting in touch with what you truly want accomplishes just that. When the wisdom that is yours speaks to you, take the message seriously, and stop preempting it.

WISDOM STORY: MEET CORBY
TURNING "WANT" INTO ACTION

Corby was a homemaker who wanted to start a business to help people in corporations adjust to the changing rules of etiquette in an increasingly diverse workplace. However, she felt she lacked the

qualifications and professional experience to do this and so she fig-
ured she could make her start with kids and use her network of
mothers to put together a class on etiquette for children. Although
this was doable and proved easy to start, it did not truly excite her.
Nonetheless, she thought it was the only logical way for her to start
building a reputation as an expert so she could eventually do what
she really wanted to do.

Corby's business didn't really take off, so after two frustrating
years, she was willing to take a chance. She started sending flyers to
companies, offering to teach classes to their employees. The response was immediate and overwhelming: she had obviously struck a
chord with what these businesspeople needed. Corby's experience
and confidence grew, and she eventually became a respected newspaper columnist on business etiquette and the proprietor of Corby
O'Connor and Company, Business Etiquette and Protocol.

Once Corby acted on what she felt she wanted—instead of just on
what she thought she could have—breakthroughs came effortlessly
for her. It sounds logical and simple, but culturally, we are deeply
rooted in making decisions based on what other people think or
expect, thus muddling what we feel and our ability to feel secure
in what we want. Anytime we fear a consequence we are operat-
ing from what others will think. No wonder it's so hard to feel and
be connected to what we truly want—it's hard to know whether we
are hearing our deepest truth or battling our coping mechanisms
for life.

FEELING SUBTLETIES

So, how do you get in touch with what you're feeling? How do you
distinguish between the subtle desires that can lead you toward accomplishing a goal easily and the sometimes overwhelmingly rational
instructions your brain sends that can lead to much more difficulty

and stress in your life? It takes practice. You can learn to feel the subtle distinctions between feelings, and then you will increase the speed at which you process information and attract positive outcomes. How you get there, however, is usually by trial and error, by deliberately and consistently paying attention to when your emotions tell you, "I want this," and your thoughts are saying, "I should do this." There are dozens of these subtleties. Let's look at a few of them.

WISDOM IN ACTION

This exercise will start you on your way to becoming more sensitive to the difference between "want" and "should"—the first subtlety we will explore.

The _____ Day

The exercise is called "The _____ Day" because you can fill your name in the blank, and the first step is to find a day that you can keep blank, or completely open.

Take a whole day and leave it free, with no plans or obligations at all. On this day, no one is to need you or demand anything of you (not even your dog), nor can you demand anything of yourself. Setting aside an entire day to do this may seem like a tall order (I know it is if you have kids). If doing this is impossible for you, you can experience a similar effect by giving yourself just a few hours of completely blank time.

Starting right at the beginning of the period you've set aside, I want you to constantly ask yourself, "What do I want?" If the answer is that you want Oreo cookies for breakfast, have them. If you want to dance around the house to loud music, terrific. If you want to play golf or curl up with a good book, do it. Whatever it is, as long as it won't hurt you or someone else, indulge!

As you physically give yourself to whatever you've told yourself you wanted, I'd like you to notice what you feel. (My clients often report feeling the joyful kind of wanting in their heart, their solar plexus area, or their stomach, or a tingling in their fingers.) There is no right answer, so just get to know your sensations for yourself.

You probably know what "should" feels like. You're anxious, bothered, perhaps confused. Some people feel it in their head, or in the solar plexus, or in the chest and neck. It doesn't matter where it registers, as long as you are now aware of the different physical sensations of "should" and "want."

Use this chart to record your observations on your _____ day.

FEELING THE SUBTLETIES

I Want   *Location of Physical Sensation*

_____   _____

_____   _____

_____   _____

_____   _____

In case any "shoulds" show up, enter them here:

I Should   *Location of Physical Sensation*

_____   _____

_____   _____

_____   _____

_____   _____

As you increase your awareness through this exercise, you won't have to think so hard about it, you'll just make quicker decisions because you are sensitive to how "want" and "should" feel.

IS IT GOOD GUILT OR BAD GUILT?

As you learn to distinguish between "want" and "should," you will probably experience one feeling that you'll have no trouble identifying: when you begin to feel what you really want and recognize how much you may have denied your wants in the past, guilt usually starts to show its all-too-familiar face. However, you'll need to distinguish good guilt from bad guilt as you let your own wisdom direct the path of your work and life. Here, we will take a closer look at the hidden messages of guilt and how to interpret them.

Good guilt is the kind that taps you on the shoulder and says, "Hey, before you do that, take a look inside to see if you will have any regret about this decision." Listening to your feelings of good guilt before you take an action will help you figure out whether you might:

- Regret taking a job in another city (or not taking it).
- Regret confronting a friend on an issue (or not doing so).
- Regret being at work instead of staying home with your kids while they are growing up.
- Regret taking five years out of your career to raise kids.

No matter how it plays out, good guilt is trying to tell you something and can help you formulate a decision that will work for you.

Bad guilt, on the other hand, is unnecessary angst delivered by an outside messenger that echoes your loudest fears. It says you are a lousy manager, a bad parent, a terrible sibling because it shamelessly compares you to an unachievable ideal.

When you notice feelings of guilt, ask yourself whether they are based on what other people will think if you don't do *x* or if you do do *y*. If so, this is not wisdom speaking to you. It's your ego sneaking in another "should." Thank it for its opinion and ignore it.

> ### GUILT.
> **Is it**
> *good* or *bad*?
>
> **What will you**
> REGRET?
>
> **Is this a**
> *want* or a *should*?

BAD GUILT IN ACTION

Peter was a top executive who came to me when he was about to fire one of his team leaders. He was feeling tremendous guilt about this move and not only was he arguing with other executives over it, he was also experiencing physical symptoms: he couldn't sleep, he had painful stomachaches, and he often caught himself clenching his jaw. He knew that letting the employee go was essential to the success of his company, but personally he felt guilty because he felt he could have done more to help this person succeed.

I explained the difference between good guilt and bad guilt to him, and asked which he was experiencing. Peter saw that his rumblings were a product of bad guilt. Using regret as a barometer, there wasn't anything compelling enough to keep him from taking action. He could say that he regretted not having tried harder, but in taking a second look that wasn't really true.

His anxiety and confusion were due to having set up a standard for himself against which he was inaccurately measuring his success as a manager. He had created an unspoken rule that he had to have the grit and leadership qualities to make *every* situation work or he wasn't "good" or capable.

I asked Peter to think about the action that was needed in this situation from a different angle. Instead of asking himself, "What *should* I do?" (fire this person), the new question Peter posed was, "What do I need to do to make my organization work?" Here the answer was: "Dismiss an employee who is keeping us from being successful." When Peter thought in terms of what he wanted—a functional, smoothly running company—his physical symptoms of stress and anxiety disappeared.

GOOD GUILT IN ACTION

Peter had been experiencing bad guilt, which can be incapacitating. Good guilt, on the other hand, has unique and positive qualities. Wendy, another client, had accepted a once-in-a-lifetime job opportunity in another city, but she could not seem to shake feelings of guilt about moving her family to a new home and asking her husband to uproot his career. When I asked Wendy to think about good guilt versus bad guilt, she saw that her true feelings had more to do with a sense of loss and regret over moving far away from her parents and extended family. Wendy realized that she deeply wanted her children to have a close relationship with their grandparents and the rest of her family. When Wendy saw how and why she might come to regret her decision, she changed her mind and turned down the job. Her husband and kids were tremendously relieved to stay put and, within a few months, an equally attractive job in the local area was offered to Wendy.

Now, what about the feelings of guilt you experience when you want to do something nice for yourself, especially if it costs money or takes time? Although I've seen more women suffer over this than men, it is by no means a women-only issue.

To find out whether this is good guilt or bad guilt, ask yourself the following questions: Will I regret doing this thing? Will I regret spending the time? Will I regret spending the money required to enjoy this delightful thing?

If paying out all that money could cause a problem for you, don't do it. But often when you consider splurging on yourself, you do have the money and you do have the time—and yet bad guilt stands in your way. What do we know about bad guilt? It's drivel, right? So, move on, pass go, and do this delicious thing.

Bad guilt tends to place you in perpetual self-doubt, making you tortuously question your desires and motivations. On the other hand, good guilt feels more like a gentle nagging or prodding, asking you to do better for yourself and your life. By identifying the source of your guilt—whether it's doing something you're liable to regret or if you're holding yourself to an impossible standard—you're likely to feel relief. Your guilt may dissipate. Whenever you feel ease melt over you or are surprised by experiencing elation, give yourself a pat on the back. You've struck gold. You've connected with wisdom.

AM I INSPIRED, OR IS IT MY EGO?

Do you know when your desire to do something is stemming from ego gratification versus when it's truly responding to inspiration from within?

Working with people who want more out of their lives, I see how so many of us are deeply affected by the celebrity culture we live in. Our idea of "making it" usually involves a lot of the money and fame we see being lavished on entertainers and sports figures. Now, nothing against thinking big, but this false vision of success can make it hard for us to set the goals and pursue the path that will truly fulfill us in life. Such cultural brainwashing causes us to question ourselves if we aim for achievements that are less grand than total physical, emotional, and financial perfection. We often think that a big goal stems from inner inspiration, when it's really just an ego-motivated attempt to prove self-worth.

This doesn't mean that everyone who has the drive to achieve great things is doing so to be famous or is trying to validate self-worth by gaining stock in others' opinions. However, it would be interesting to see how many such stardom seekers would still pursue their purported goals if there was little pay or recognition involved. The few that would stick around are inspired—the rest are getting a need met. I am not saying that the desire to be famous is a "bad" thing. I only mean to show you which feelings and inner motivations will help you attain ease and satisfaction.

I've actually struggled with this myself. As I address larger audiences through writing and appearing on television, my family, friends, and colleagues often say, "Hey, you're a celebrity now!" It never occurred to me that that was the case. I felt it was more their projection of what being successful means, that success is defined by being on TV and writing books. I'd be a hypocrite if I said the attention wasn't fun. However, I have asked myself many times if I would still do this work if it did not keep me in the public eye. The answer is yes, I would (at least at this point in my life, and that's the only vantage point each of us has).

One of my clients is an Emmy Award–winning television personality. He had worked for one or two of the major networks earlier in his career, but he chose to focus on creating and hosting educational programming for public television so he could have the quality of life he wanted. This man was completely sure that he was following his inspiration, not his ego. He was making great use of his talents and a contribution to society, but he still felt a twinge of angst every time someone said, "You know, you should really be one of those guys on NBC." These people were hinting he was "less than" because he put his own priorities before ego.

The kind of thinking these friends illustrate is exactly what keeps us checking somewhere outside of ourselves for answers. This can set us up to be a bottomless pit of need for external validation. Hey, we're human, a need for external validation is going to happen once in a while, but you can save yourself a lot of strife if you learn to feel the difference between ego and inspiration. When feelings of insecurity strike, keep in mind what ego feels like and what inspiration feels like. Inspiration comes from within, and ego depends on others to feel at ease and satisfied. Inspiration will feel less tumultuous than ego.

IS IT PASSION OR ADRENALINE?

Beating a competitor, speaking in public, trying to take care of thirty items on your to-do list in a single day, coaching your kid's Little

League game to a win against all odds—all these things make you feel charged up. It's a temporary high that keeps you "pumped up" and raring to go, but often leaves you empty and exhausted when the "rush" dies down.

On the other hand, starting something from the ground up, losing track of time in the abandon of a project, stretching beyond what you feel capable of in the name of a good cause—these efforts can tire you as well, but here the exhaustion is more likely to resemble the satisfying weariness you experience after a long hike in the great outdoors.

Of the two paragraphs above, the first describes activities fueled by adrenaline; the second, activities fueled by passion.

The key to distinguishing passion from adrenaline lies in understanding its source. Remember, we are memorizing feelings in order to hear the body's wisdom more clearly and act on what we feel. What does boundless enthusiasm feel like? What does an adrenaline rush feel like? Which one is more sustainable? Passion is; an adrenaline rush lets you down hard and you need to muster another rush to sustain it. Watching the ebb and flow of your energy level will help you distinguish between the two.

Adrenaline excites us—excitement makes us feel good—so we stick with it. But when it comes down to relying on your body for wisdom's clues, adrenaline will fool you every time. It causes you to feel such a rush that you could mistake it for the voice of the Big One himself. However, adrenaline lies. It's a high that makes you feel bigger and more capable than you really are. When you make decisions under the influence of an adrenaline rush, you are doing so based on a short-lived feeling that could leave you frustrated down the road. Caught up in the hormonal charge, you may overextend yourself, promise more than you can deliver, or say yes when you really mean to say no.

We talked earlier about the way adrenaline can wear down our system and how its insidious nature makes it hard to decipher. It feels like passion and excitement, but it isn't. Sheila's story will help to illustrate this point.

GETTING PAST GIVING

Sheila, the mother of one of my best friends, has been a mentor to me and is someone I have long admired. She is someone who thrives on helping others. People seek her counsel or ask for her help on projects because she is known for possessing deep wisdom and insight, as well as for having the patience of a saint.

Sheila came to me for coaching after battling breast cancer (having already battled thyroid cancer). Although our main agenda was to build her small business, Sheila's health was frequently addressed. She was often exhausted, but was unable to see how paying attention to the needs of others debilitated her. In fact, Sheila thought helping others propped her up. When she felt needed, her adrenaline kicked in and she would go on a high, spreading the fairy dust of her goodwill and saving the day whenever she could.

Through our coaching, Sheila began to see she could be just as helpful to others without depleting her own energy. She learned that if she wanted to say no, she could. She realized that she was not ultimately responsible for everyone who wanted her help and that by saying no, she might actually end up being more helpful to these people in the long run by forcing them to help themselves.

As hard as it was, Sheila admitted to needing the high she got from being needed. She started to feel the difference between experiencing an adrenaline rush and a true desire to help someone else. She reevaluated the priorities in her life, separating adrenaline from genuine passion. Yes, some people were disappointed when their "savior" wasn't readily available, but to this day, Sheila remains cancer-free—something she attributes to learning how to say no to overpromising, needing to be needed, and adrenaline rushes.

IS IT AN OPPORTUNITY
OR A SEDUCTION?

Have you ever been offered something that is too good to be true? An incredible business opportunity, a free trip, an out-of-the-blue invitation to attend a ritzy event? When presented with opportunities like these, most of us will hear a small voice in the back of our minds asking, "What's the catch?"

That little voice is probably trying to get you to pay attention to another key distinction to watch for as you uncover your true "wants." Often, something you want, such as saying yes to a seemingly great opportunity, is not a true opportunity, but rather a seduction. The sooner you listen to that voice, the easier your life will be.

True opportunities benefit all parties involved. You will feel a sense of ease and expanded possibility when presented with one. A seduction, on the other hand, usually means that you get something out of it temporarily, but the party offering it to you benefits a lot more. You get used as the offeror's needs are met. A seduction usually does not feel free and unrestrained. You may sense tension or doubt about the other party's intentions.

When you can feel the difference between an opportunity and a seduction, you can prevent yourself from expending unnecessary energy in pursuit of a disappointing reward. Your body's clues—the feeling that something is not quite right—is your natural wisdom speaking to you.

For example, my client Marlee met Brian, a fellow consultant, at a conference. Brian was looking for a new partner for a venture he was starting up. Although Marlee had a feeling immediately that he was not to be fully trusted, he also seemed genuine, informed, connected, and savvy. Marlee ignored her misgivings because she could not point to any specific reason not to get involved with this man.

It took two years and a lot of legal paperwork to get Marlee out of that relationship. Sadly, Brian's venture turned out to be a bust. Marlee lost time, money, and a great deal of emotional energy in extracting herself from her professional relationship with him. Despite our coaching, she had not been willing to trust what she ultimately knew was true until she had plenty of evidence that she had been seduced and not the recipient of an opportunity. Unfortunately, by then, the damage had been done.

ARE YOU CERTAIN OR ARE YOU INFATUATED?

Knowing the difference between certainty and infatuation is another subtle distinction that can help us come up with a clearer path to what we most want from our lives. For me the word "infatuation" always conjures up an intense schoolgirl crush, the kind that was unrelenting, all-encompassing, and totally intoxicating. A feeling and a stream of consciousness that consumes the days and nights, until you're unaware of anything else. What's wrong with that? Nothing—except it's just a big old waste of time and something you'll later write off in the name of experience.

Certainty, on the other hand, is something you can take action on. It dictates a direction. Although certainty is not completely concrete, it sure beats indecision. Let's stick to romantic relationships here for a moment, since I started talking about schoolgirl crushes. When you are infatuated with someone, your family and friends never seem to be wholeheartedly accepting of the relationship.

However, if you are certain you've found the love of your life, even when others aren't as sure of your choice, they generally leave you to your own devices. It doesn't mean they don't care enough to intercede, but rather that people feel awe at wisdom. Even if your family and friends can't see what you see in your beloved, they respect that there is something you know that they don't. They are willing to respect your certainty, even if they would have seen through you if you'd merely been infatuated. It's easy for caring, objective bystanders to see through infatuation. It bothers them. Infatuation suggests an absence of sound judgment and people react to the insanity of this.

What does all this mean for your life's blueprint? It's important for you to learn to feel the difference between infatuation and certainty. If you are considering a job offer across the country, ask yourself if it is the right job for you or whether you are infatuated with the idea of moving to a new city and starting over. If you are thinking of starting your own business, ask yourself whether it is because you know with certainty that you want to be your own boss, with all the responsibility for the success or failure of the business, or if you are just in love with the idea of being able to say to the neighbors that you work for yourself.

We've looked at only six subtleties, but now that you've learned to distinguish among them, some themes are starting to emerge. Most of the less desirable feelings are based in fear or a perception of something missing. The fear could be a fear of consequences or a fear of not having or being enough. There will usually be an external measurement at the root of the fear and it will probably be emotionally "noisy." There would probably be a noticeable absence of peace and ease, the signs that you've connected with your own wisdom.

A wisdom-based decision will never be dictated by fear. You may have to overcome fear (which we talked about in chapter 3), but the truth of what direction to take will always be rooted in courage, love, integrity, and goodness. The big questions will be: Are you worth it? Will you give it to yourself? Will you do what you know is right for you?

WISDOM WRITING

Spend time writing down how you have felt the difference between good guilt and bad guilt, inspiration and ego, passion and adrenaline, opportunity and seduction, and certainty and inspiration. (You already wrote about the difference between "want" and "should" on p. 69.) Give specific reference to people, places, and details that will remind you of times when you have felt these subtleties. Record any lessons you may have learned, and how you will recognize these feelings in the future. When you pay more attention to how you feel in situations instead of relying on your linear, logical judgment, you will have quicker access to the answers that will make a difference in attaining what you want.

YOUR BODY AS COMPASS: "THE ZONE"

Once you have learned to identify these subtleties of feeling, you are ready to recognize the not-so-subtle feeling of entering "the zone." In sports, "the zone" is the place where athletes feel connected to a force that propels them to the perfect game. They report an ease and a lack of effort, even though they are fully present in the moment. It's as if time stands still and the hyperawareness of the moment creates a dreamlike state. In that suspended reality mind, body, and spirit come together effortlessly to perform flawlessly.

There is a similar zone with wisdom and when you enter it for the first time, you have a physical feeling that things are right, as if the stars have aligned in your favor. Your inner compass is pointing to true north. You will always remember this feeling because it marks a moment when you put yourself on the course to your life blueprint. You've entered the zone.

Wisdom is the zone of decision making. The feeling you are looking for is that same ease that the well-trained athlete can achieve. You become the well-trained player when you allow yourself to know how you feel. When you enter the wisdom zone, you may feel a lightness, as if all the heaviness of your life were dissipating. You may experience a feeling of expansion: your brain may feel as if it had expanded, your heart and lungs too. These are feelings of tapping into wisdom.

FEELING YOUR WAY TO THE TRUTH

Marianne was a client who worked in a large family business for many years. She liked her work, but felt that her talents were not fully used in this job and, worse, her opinions were constantly lost in the family pecking order.

For a long time Marianne had wanted to start her own business. Through our work together, she was able to overcome her fear of upsetting her family by striking out on her own. Marianne endured nearly being disowned by her family and their harsh criticism. Still, she felt a lightness about her decision that gave her confirmation that she was doing the right thing. It felt surreal, and she was amazed at her level of calm. If she wanted to, she could conjure up as much turmoil as her family was experiencing, but she knew it wasn't what she was really feeling. Instead, Marianne was in touch with a feeling of expansion and freedom that started in her solar plexus and reverberated through her body.

Marianne has been successfully running her own business for more than two years. She can still measure the feelings to know she is staying on track.

WRAPPING IT UP
WITH THE COACH

In this chapter you learned how to get beyond your thoughts and let your feelings tell you what to do. You saw how to:

- Continually take care of and eliminate what keeps you too busy to feel.
- Keep your focus on how your priorities are reflected in your life.
- Feel the difference between "want" and "should."

- Pay attention to subtleties in emotion: the distinctions between your wisdom and your coping mechanisms (inspirations vs. ego, passion vs. adrenaline, etc.).
- Feel the zone and use it to know when your actions are wisdom-based.

MAKE A SIMPLE CONTRACT

FOCUS ON THE PRESENT

So much of our life is geared toward future achievements and successes that it's often hard to remember that it is the present we inhabit. We are forced to be "big girls" and "big boys" before we are ready. We are trained to think about college before we've finished our freshman year of high school. We are asked our thoughts on marriage before we've dated someone for six months. The list goes on, but the point is that our success is often measured by where we are headed instead of where we actually are.

Although there's nothing wrong with planning, visualizing, and looking ahead, many of us struggle to reach the future without really paying attention to what is going on in the present. My clients most often come to me wanting to create a great future, and they are startled to learn that the way to do this is by taking care of the present first.

We begin our work by facing the truth about what a client's life circumstances are telling her. If these are not what she wants them to be (and they usually are not), we then work diligently to change her life focus, reexamine her priorities, and come up with solutions to her present-day problems. Taking care of all these things releases a tremendous amount of negative energy, after which attracting a great future is easier.

For example, a woman's magazine asked me to help one of its readers, Dana, achieve the goal of getting in the best physical shape of her life. She had been given a professionally designed exercise schedule and a routine, but she was always too exhausted to follow this regime. When we began working together, it was clear to me that she was hoping we could skip over the reality of the present (that she was exhausted) and magically get her into the best shape of her life. Hhhhmmm.

Focusing on the present, Dana and I discovered that she didn't leave the office until quite late every night. In addition, she did not eat well or drink enough water during the day, and she didn't get enough sleep. To solve these problems, we created an ideal schedule that allowed her time to include meals and adequate rest. It meant delegating more at work and being ruthless with her time. I knew that Dana's motivation and ability to change her future could develop only if she took better care of herself in the present.

It is just impossible to reach a future ideal goal if the present is not set up to support it. Yet we continue to squander our present in yearning for a better future. "If I only had this [or that], things would be better," we say. Or, "If I can just make some money to cover this credit card debt, then I'll be all right." Or, "When I find a mate, I'll be happy."

Whatever the case may be, keep in mind that the fastest way out is *through*. This chapter is about facing the truth and doing something about it. The results may be even better than what you were spending your precious present wishing for.

WHAT IS A SIMPLE CONTRACT?

Facing the truth and doing something about it involves making a pact with yourself that says you will do whatever it takes to make your life work in the present. I call this pact a simple contract. This contract means you are willing to give up big goals and fantasies of salvation in order to deal with what is true about your life now, and make it work. Marianne Williamson, lecturer and author of the best-selling *A Return to Love,* once said, "Our only job is to be an example of a life that is working." A life that is working is one in which your complaints are at a minimum and, although everything may not be perfect, it works. You have more than enough money, more than enough love and support, more than enough satisfaction out of the things that you do and the company you keep.

When you make a simple contract, you will start by taking care of the "real matters" at hand. These real matters are those things that are not working for you on a daily basis. Those things could include a relationship that gives you trouble, a money life that is less than stellar, a job you hate, or anything else that plagues you and doesn't seem to get resolved on its own.

The simple contract does not apply only to people in dire straits; it is useful for every single person who is not happy, regardless of his or her income level or social status. Even people at the top of their game sometimes suffer from wishing it would all go away tomorrow. Such fruitless yearning can plague anyone who has neglected their own wisdom. The yearning may be a result of neglecting the signs that you need a change, a rest, a resolution to a problem, or an antidote to the situation.

To make a simple contract with yourself, first look at all aspects of your life to determine what is working and what is not. This is not the time to dream big and yearn for the ideal. It is not the time to set goals. It is the time to evaluate what is true now.

Ask yourself: What makes me happy? My home? My job? My family? What is not satisfying? Is something or someone causing me pain? Am I underpaid? Do I want to be in better physical shape? Do I want a better relationship with my parent, my spouse, or my child?

Making a simple contract does not require that you have solutions to the less desirable elements of your life, just that you take stock of them.

EVALUATE YOUR LIFE

Use this list to evaluate what works and what doesn't in your immediate world. Copy the list onto a piece of paper. For each item, write yes next to each item if you are satisfied with how it is working in your life, or no if you are not satisfied. If you are sometimes satisfied, write no because there is probably some work for you to do on this item. It may also help to ask yourself, Does this work for me or against me? Does it contribute positively to my life or negatively?

Feel free to add any items I have not included that are of relevance to you. You will be instructed on what to do with this information later in the chapter.

Relationships
____ My spouse or significant other
____ My child/children
____ My parents
____ My siblings
____ My friends

Possessions
____ My clothes
____ My appliances
____ My work tools
____ My "toys"
____ My furniture

Career/Work
____ My coworkers
____ The culture, tone, atmosphere
____ My workload
____ My job description/ responsibilities

Environment
____ My home
____ My office
____ My outside view
____ My car
____ My bedroom

Health and Well-being
____ My emotional life
____ My body
____ My diet
____ My habits
____ My indulgences

Money
____ My money-management habits
____ My income
____ My spending
____ My savings

Activities
____ Social
____ Religious
____ Spiritual
____ Leisure
____ Volunteer
____ School

WISDOM STORY: MEET MITCH

PUTTING THE SIMPLE CONTRACT INTO ACTION

Mitch liked fast cars, fast women, fast deals, and fast food—the faster, the better. He considered himself a mover and a shaker. By the outside world's standards, he was successful, but in private he admitted to me that he felt lonely and disconnected from others. He wouldn't dream of letting anyone in his circle know how he felt, however, because he presumed he needed to keep up his image as a savvy, together guy.

Nonetheless, Mitch had chosen to work with me to examine how he managed his life and to see how he could be more satisfied with the life he led.

Filling out the checklist above, Mitch recognized that first of all, he had to improve his eating habits and his physical health. Due to his flamboyant lifestyle, he was out of shape and feeling sluggish. He also found that he needed to pay more attention to how he dealt with money; since he was rapidly running up huge credit card debt. Finally, it was clear he had to do some work on his relationships, because his conscience was bothering him.

Mitch made a simple contract, committing to take action on what was not working in his life and turn it around. He began by reconciling some old relationships and mending some old hurts with past lovers. A great weight was lifted off him by doing so. He further increased his feeling of well-being by banishing junk foods from his diet and resumed exercising.

Clearing up his debt was a much slower process, but just knowing he was taking action toward doing so contributed to the increased vitality he felt. Mitch experienced not just heightened energy but a sense of ease and an increased peace of mind. He began to attract new and interesting people into his life, people who shared his new interests and healthier lifestyle. In turn, these new friendships brought a fresh set of possibilities and opportunities into his life.

Within just a few months, Mitch changed from a dissatisfied mover and shaker to someone who was enjoying a richer, more fully connected life on many levels. He no longer cared to keep up a pretentious image. He didn't have to. His life was beginning to work and he no longer had to live a lie.

THE TRUTH WILL HELP YOU TAKE ACTION

When you make the simple contract, you have finally listened to the truth about the circumstances in your life, and you have no choice but to take responsibility for them. It takes so much energy to deny the truth and hide from it that once you admit what is so, you feel an immediate release and a burst of renewed positive energy. The truth offers you wisdom (even when it isn't positive), because once the truth is spoken, you are free to take action. You are free to change. You are free to create forward motion in your life.

The tricky thing about the truth is that it is always changing. Once spoken, what is true for you today could turn out to be no longer true tomorrow or the next day. For example, if you share your feelings of hurt with a friend or a co-worker whose words have wounded you, the hurt might disappear, just by having spoken it. Once you are no longer experiencing hurt, you are living a different truth. Admitting what is true in a way that does not hurt others allows the possibility of a wise solution to or even the transformation of a negative situation.

One of my colleagues spent years denying he was bankrupt, living painfully cloaked in shame and deceit. Once he admitted the truth of his circumstances to himself and the people around him, he discovered that the consequences of declaring bankruptcy were not nearly as harsh as he had feared. He was then able to close down his business with dignity, speak to his creditors openly, and begin a new and better life.

Our tendency is to avoid difficult truths, trying strategy after strategy to do so, only to be left feeling empty or frustrated even if we succeed in covering up our reality because it becomes a hollow victory. The underlying problem is still there. When you make a simple contract and tell the truth about your life, you have allowed your life to tell you what it needs from you, instead of you telling your life what you need from it. When we are not satisfied with our lives, no matter how outwardly perfect they look, this is what is going on.

We cannot override the truth. No matter how hard we try, we cannot. You can spend a lifetime trying, but in the end, it will have been a much harder life. Deal with what is true.

WISDOM STORY: MEET PHILIPPE

THE FREEDOM TO CHANGE COMES FROM TRUTH

Philippe was the executive chef at a five-star hotel in New Orleans. His company was grateful for his years of service, but he was concerned that he was not changing with the times. Deep down, Philippe knew that his managers were growing impatient with him and that his job was in danger if he did not make some changes, but this truth was very hard for him to face.

Philippe was a very proud man who at first found it hard to trust me with his private thoughts and struggles. Once trust was established, it became clear to me that he treated his staff very poorly, showing little patience, cultural sensitivity, or faith in their ability to carry out his orders. He micromanaged and basically ran the kitchen as a dictatorship. He resisted becoming computer-literate, thus further hampering his effectiveness. He worked ridiculously long hours, letting weeks pass before he would reluctantly take a day off. This put a tremendous strain on his relationship with his wife and seriously cut into the time he longed to spend with his young grandchild. The stress and isolation of his life was taking its toll and, after years of abstinence, he had started drinking again.

As hard as it was for Philippe to share these things with a stranger, he felt tremendous relief when, with my help, he made a simple contract. Admitting his difficulties was enough to start improving. Admitting he was drinking made him feel accountable enough to give up alcohol without additional help. He got himself a computer coach and even let one of his staff show him how to do the ordering and accounting electronically. Learning from someone his junior helped him gain respect for this young staff member, which in turn aided Philippe in slowly delegating responsibilities and giving instructions in a more empowering way. In time, his kitchen became a well-run, friendly place.

Before committing to the simple contract, Philippe used to go home grumpy and was unable to engage in conversations that required problem solving or intimacy. Now he was able to ask for the time he needed for himself to decompress. He was thus more equipped to engage with his loved ones in a way that fueled their relationships. The new intimacy and peace he'd helped to create made home a place he looked forward to being and a place he enjoyed.

After a few months, Philippe was asked to be part of the launch team for several new hotels his company was building across the country. All of Philippe's forward motion and improvement started only after he admitted the truth about his present and resolved to change it.

YOU ALREADY KNOW
WHAT NEEDS TO BE DONE

If you are like most of the people I have worked with, you already know what needs to change in your life. You don't need me to tell you, any more than do my clients, who simply can't bring themselves to make the necessary changes or have convinced themselves that they don't know how to make them.

By now, you've taken a good hard look at what is working in your life and what is not. I hope that you've been able to be truthful with yourself during this process. All you need is a little push to get you headed toward doing something about what you've discovered.

WISDOM WRITING

This exercise will show you how you already know what needs to be done in your life.

Return to the checklist in which you identified the areas in your life that were and weren't working (pp. 87–88). In your wisdom journal or computer file, create a separate page or heading for each area in the checklist: relationships, environment, possessions, health and well-being, career/work, money, and activities. Focus on the aspects in each group that you have already determined are not working.

For each item, ask yourself the following Wisdom Access Questions:

- "What do I need to *know* about solving my issues with my _____ [money, relationships, etc.]?"
- "What do I need to *do* about my _____ [environment, activities, etc.]?"

Pose each question, take a deep breath and then write down the answer spontaneously. Don't think too much about your response. Try to frame your answers as if the issues themselves were speaking to you.

For example, if you are having trouble in a particular relationship, respond to the question as if you were the person with whom you are having the problem. It might sound like this: "What you need to know is that I'm sorry I broke your trust.

What you need to do is forgive me." Or if your savings plan is not working, your money itself may speak: "What you need to do is save 10 percent of every check."

When you are done, go back and use a highlighter to mark things that translate into direct action items. For example, if your money told you, "It's time to invest," highlight those words.

Then, make a list of action items from each heading. These lists become part of your simple contract. These are the simple goals and actions that will matter in excavating the blueprint for your best life.

DOING THE WORK

Commit now to do whatever it takes to be responsible in every area of your life. This is, of course, easier said than done. I suggest you start by concentrating only on one area, and don't go on to tackle another until you are ready. Be compassionate with yourself. By this, I'm not saying you should be lazy, just that you need to be kind to yourself as you deal with the challenges of perfecting your present.

Once again, the only way out is *through*. This is why we did all that work on understanding what you're feeling in the last chapter. If you can feel the truth, you can tell it and once it's told, action must be taken.

Nothing clears the way to your best life faster than doing the immediate work that your life requires. There are no shortcuts. To me, the following story (which a friend sent me) perfectly illustrates this.

Words of Wisdom: Leaving the Moth to Do the Work

A man found a cocoon of an emperor moth and took it home to watch the moth emerge. One day, a small opening appeared in the cocoon and he watched as the moth struggled to force its body through that tiny hole. After several hours, though, it seemed to stop making progress, as if it had gotten as far as it could and could go no farther. It was stuck.

Then the man decided to help the moth, so he took a pair of scissors and snipped off the remaining bit of the cocoon. This allowed the moth to emerge easily. But it had a swollen body and small, shriveled wings.

While the man continued to watch the moth, expecting its wings to enlarge and expand at any moment to be able to support its body, this never happened. The little moth spent the rest of its life crawling around with a swollen body and shriveled wings. It was never able to fly.

What the man, in his kindness, did not understand was that the restricting cocoon and the struggle required for the moth to get through the opening were nature's way of forcing fluid from the body of the moth into its wings, so that it would be ready for flight once it achieved its freedom from the cocoon. Freedom and flight could come only after struggle.

By depriving the moth of a struggle, he deprived the moth of health.

How many times have we wanted to take the quick way out of struggles, to take scissors and snip off our difficulties in order to be free of them? How many times have we wanted to do this for our kids, loved ones, and colleagues? We need to remember, however, that it is through our trials and struggles that we are strengthened.

WISDOM STORY: MEET DANIELLE

DUKING IT OUT WITH THE PRESENT TO GET TO A GREAT FUTURE

Danielle, a photographer, had always had money problems. She tended to make promises in her business that she couldn't keep, and her unhappy clients would refuse to pay her. Danielle would then borrow from family and friends, but be unable to make good on her debts. She often resorted to lying and cheating to get by.

I never officially worked with Danielle as a client, so I could only watch from the sidelines, but what I saw was remarkable. One day, she decided to get her life in order. She did so in very small steps, fighting her natural tendencies all the way. But despite her efforts to show up on time, be diligent about her work, and finally open a bank account to keep track of her money, life soon began to test her resolve. Danielle lost her wallet and had to chase down all the pieces of her life. She got kicked out of her apartment for her previous trespasses of not paying rent and had to move in with a friend. Many people were sick of her antics and did not believe she had changed, and although they turned their backs on her, she did not falter. She worked to save money and contribute to her friend's household expenses. She had finally decided to deal with what was true in her life and grow from it instead of dishonoring herself by avoiding it.

After a year, Danielle rented her own living space and began to see her reputation as a photographer rise again. She mended some of her old friendships and paid off her debts. It took a few more years before she felt on top of her finances and began to breathe easy again. Even though she would be the first to tell you that she would have been headed for disaster if she had not decided to face reality, she is grateful for the accomplishment of being able to say she turned her own life around.

Danielle did this by admitting the truth and doing the work to turn around what she had done step by little step. To escape from the whirlwind that had become her life, she had to lower her expectations and make her focus very narrow and very simple. In effect, she made a simple contract and it all began with keeping her word.

KEEPING YOUR WORD

Telling the truth about your life's circumstances is only one part of the simple contract. Keeping your word once you've given it is also a crucial component of the contract. Keeping your word means staying true to the promises you make, especially to yourself.

Believe it or not, we tend to betray ourselves even more than we do others. It is to ourselves that we must first begin to give our word and keep it. This means not only telling the truth, but also learning to make promises that we can keep in the first place.

Having faith, or trust in ourselves is absolutely essential to anything we want to accomplish in life, and we lose that trust every time we do not keep a promise to ourselves. If you broke as many promises with a small child as you do with yourself, you would not be surprised if the child didn't trust you and walked on eggshells around you. Similarly, breaking your own promises to yourself erodes your self-esteem. It deafens you to wisdom.

Whatever you neglect to honor—the promise to work out, eat well, save money, spend less, be more patient, or play with your kids more, or any other vow that matters to you—these betrayals of self, and the associated guilt and shame we often feel, become an undetectable poison under our skin.

The fact is that, although we live with the false sense that the core of our worldly success is our goals and being better and smarter, the true work is being able to trust ourselves implicitly. When you can do this, you have confidence in yourself, confidence that shines through and acts as a beacon for success.

The secret to keeping your promises is to simplify. Make your every promise small enough to be doable. Don't make an all-encompassing promise that all but sets you up for failure. Instead of saying "I won't eat anything fattening today," say "I will keep my word to watch my diet today and make conscious choices about what I eat." You can still choose to blow your calorie limit on an ice cream cone, but you do so consciously. Instead of saying, "I won't raise my voice at work anymore," say "I will keep my cool today"—or for the next hour, or whatever time period is short enough so that you can keep your promise to yourself.

Small promises allow you to be someone of your word. Your word is the glue that holds your best life together, and every broken promise to yourself is a crack in the foundation that supports your life. If you don't keep promises you will not be punished or suffer some grave fate, but it will make it harder for you. You may not be conscious of where you are breaking promises, but if you feel life is not treating you as you'd like, take a look at where you are not keeping your word. Then start keeping your word, or simplify what you promise so you *can* keep it.

BECOME THE OBSERVER OF YOUR LIFE

In order for you to make and keep the simple contract, you'll also need to become the observer of it. Just as an actor would observe someone to portray them, observing your life allows you to live in it fully.

In his book *The E-Myth,* Michael Gerber describes how a business owner, in order to be most successful, must work not only *in* his business but also work *on* his business. As your coach, I ask you to do the same for your life. You can't just be *in* your life, you must work *on* it.

To do this, take the time to pay attention to your life instead of just surviving each day. Your world is giving you feedback and clues that you need to stop to observe. It is showing you the way, and any obstacles are part of that journey. By observing your life as if you were outside it, you accelerate positive change because you learn more quickly about yourself and your life.

To observe your own life requires learning how to be an observer of all life. It also requires some of the detachment (not taking things personally) that we explored in chapter 3. You must step back and take cues from the world around you.

WORDS OF WISDOM:
LEARNING FROM TREES

A dear coaching colleague, Julia Olalla, once asked, "We study the trees, but what do we learn from them?" In answer, I would quote Reynold Feldman, from his book, *Wisdom: Daily Reflections for a New Era.* "Trees," he says, "instinctively grow toward the sky. They also have long lives and the resilience to stand their ground, literally and figuratively, through all kinds of weather. Deep roots surely have something to do with it." Feldman observes how trees are the quintessential servants, creating oxygen for all to breathe without asking for anything in return. Through his observation of trees, Feldman recognized the need to be sure in himself and to serve others as well. He turned his observations into wisdom he could use in his life.

You, too, can learn much about yourself and your life through this one simple aspect of nature.

Observing life doesn't mean you sit in the spectator's booth watching it pass you by. It means you are willing to learn from everything around you. It means you are willing to not have the answers, willing to ask for help, willing to do whatever it takes to make your life work, and willing to marvel at what results.

Being the observer of your life gives you the perspective that can cause a level of recognition and awareness that may very well trigger a quantum leap in what you can accomplish. For example, when I was trying to conceive my next book after publishing *Take Yourself to the Top,* I was stuck coming up with an idea. There were so many ways to frame how coaching affected people's lives and many other people writing about it. The more I pondered my dilemma, the less access I seemed to have to an answer.

Finally, I pulled back and observed. I allowed myself to not have the answer. Instead, I watched myself as I worked; I watched my clients; I studied their lives and the results they got from our work.

Suddenly, what I needed to do became clear. My job was to help others access the wisdom they already had that was designed to lead them to opportunity and satisfaction. With amazing speed, wisdom flew to the top in everything I did. Clients and students responded with such enthusiasm that it became undeniable that wisdom was to be my next book's focus. The speed and momentum I experienced in making this decision is what I mean by quantum leaps. It can happen to you too, if you stand back and observe your life for a moment or two.

WISDOM IN ACTION

Use the next day of your life as a chance to observe your own life and life in general. Keeping TV, radio, and other noisy distractions to a minimum, for the next twenty-four hours, try the following:

- Don't pipe in at every conversation.
- Daydream a little.
- Watch your kids as they play (or fight).
- Notice nature.
- Study human behavior (your own or someone else's).
- Let other people "win," just be an observer.

When the day is done, see what impression is left on you. Write down answers to these questions:

- What did I learn? Did I notice anything I wouldn't have if I hadn't been trying?
- Was there an "aha"? If so, what was it?
- Did anything in particular stand out? Did I notice my own actions more, or those of others?
- What insights did I have about myself or life in general? Did the observant approach I took today help me see the world differently or more clearly?

Don't fabricate realizations. Just let them float to the surface.

WRAPPING IT UP WITH THE COACH

The simple contract is the crux of the Doing, a step that cannot be skipped in the process of living your best life. It will help you get to a point where your life works, even at the simplest level, where goal setting and daydreaming become pleasurable games instead of desperate odysseys in search of self-worth. Self-worth reveals itself readily once you keep your commitment to the simple contract.

"Righting" every area of your life, admittedly, will take some work on your part. I trust that you know you can find any information you need. Get on the Internet, buy some of the books I recommend in Appendix 3, hire a coach, or ask a friend. Just like we talked about humor mentors earlier in this book, look for people who can mentor you on the life area you are not strong in. People are the vehicle by which our success comes to us. Ask, ask, ask. Asking for help is like telling the truth. It releases you from the strain of the lie. Just do it.

Let's review the steps to creating and honoring the simple contract:

- Focus on the present, not the future.
- Tell the truth in order to determine what is working and what is not working.
- Make a simple contract to clean up everything in your life that does not work.
- Do the work.
- Keep your word to yourself.
- Become the observer of your own life and learn from it.

DISCOVER YOUR

LUCRATIVE PURPOSE

W HAT DO YOU DO?" IT SEEMS AS THOUGH EVERY CONVERSA-
tion with a new acquaintance gets to this question sooner or
later—usually sooner. Whether you work at home or in an office,
whether you bring in no income for your daily efforts or can boast of
a seven-figure salary, the topic of "what you do" is inescapable in our
culture. To put it another way, when was the last time someone asked,
"Who are you? What is your unique purpose in the world?" Ha!

When we talk about making our life work, as we did in the last
chapter, how we earn a living and what we are meant to do with our
lives is bound to come up for examination. Ours is a "doing" culture.
We identify ourselves by our accomplishments and by how much doing we can squeeze into a day. We pass that attitude on to our kids as
we encourage them to commit to an abundance of lessons, team
sports, clubs, play dates, and other activities.

We are not necessarily flawed by being part of a doing culture,
and no one can blame us for taking a hearty bite out of life. However,
being in constant motion does cause us to take the more physically
tiring route to personal satisfaction.

This chapter is about learning to get better at defining ourselves
by who we are, rather than by what we do. Defining ourselves in this
way makes it easier to manage being part of a doing culture. More

important, our doing becomes more significant. This shift—from getting our identity from what we do, to getting it from who we are—is a big step toward the unfolding of the life we truly desire.

PURPOSEFUL DOING

I can't think of a single person I know who has not asked herself why she is here, what her purpose is, or what she can uniquely contribute to make this world a better place. For some people, it's just a matter of wondering how to fill their days with something besides routine obligations and mundane chores. Others are more concerned with meaningful self-expression. Toward this goal, some of us volunteer in our communities, others work at influential careers, and still others feel raising children well is their best contribution. But, despite our best intentions, so many of us still don't quite feel fulfilled.

We spend the majority of our waking hours working in one way or another, but we don't feel rewarded by our efforts. We spend more time and mental and physical energy on that portion of our lives than anything else, and we make the mistake of giving more time to what we "do" to find an ever-elusive payoff. Whether you are a workaholic corporate type or a stay-at-home parent, I would bet that your working hours are disproportionate to your off-duty time.

The truth is, most of us suffer to make a living and that is a waste of our potential. Even with all the choices we have today, polls show that half of us would change our careers if given the chance. A paycheck is not enough anymore—we want to make a difference. We want to know that what we do matters. We just need a little help to make us realize that we *can* have both, that we can trade in our less-than-satisfying work for deeply fulfilling work. We all have the ability to live out what I call our lucrative purpose.

Identifying your lucrative purpose can bring great clarity to the focus of your life, allowing you to experience a fullness and satisfaction that does not depend on effort, long-range planning, goal setting, goal accomplishing, or financial gain. It is the identification and recognition of who you are that can lead to the all-important impact on the world that you crave. Your lucrative purpose is already imprinted on your soul; it's part of your life blueprint.

Once it is recognized, responding to your lucrative purpose requires acceptance of its existence and commitment to its good use. At a recent seminar, a Miami woman stood up and said, "I always identified myself by what I did. I was a dental assistant, but I'd grown to hate it and have felt very lost as to what I'm supposed to do with my life." I asked her what she felt her greatest natural ability was and she replied, "Helping other people in getting a task done." As these words left her mouth, she realized this innate talent of hers could be of use in many other potentially satisfying careers. "I am not limited to being a dental assistant," she said. "I can assist in so many different industries to make money—the possibilities are endless!" What I saw here was someone who shifted the importance of being an assistant from *what* she did to *who* she was. She enjoys assisting, is fulfilled by it, and does not have to limit where or how she acts as an assistant.

Over the years of working with clients, I have noticed that when people get a sense of their natural abilities in terms of who they are instead of what they do, they naturally begin to feel a sense of purpose that allows them to turn their work into something they love by making minimal changes. They easily become enthusiastic about what they do. Since they are excited about their work and feel useful, they are making a huge contribution and they feel fulfilled while also earning a living.

Though I call this your lucrative purpose, it applies to your life in a much larger context than simply making a living. "Lucrative" describes not only financial wealth but the other riches that you can obtain, such as a sense of well-being, an abundance of love and support in your life, an awe at the coincidences that show up to take care of your needs, or the satisfaction of knowing you make a difference in the world. It is this kind of lucrative income that distinguishes the happy-go-lucky trash collector from the miserable millionaire executive.

Honoring what is innate and inherent to you is the easiest path to a sense of purpose and satisfaction. And remaining truthful to your lucrative purpose is possible no matter what job you hold. By initiating more projects, sharing your opinions and ideas more readily, and redesigning your schedule, all with a focus on what you do best and your purpose, your vitality is heightened. Whatever you do becomes more enjoyable.

Whether you choose to commit your lucrative purpose to being the means by which you earn your keep, or you decide to make it just one part of your daily life, your lucrative purpose has the potential to move your life to unexpected places and even monetary gain.

MISINTERPRETING YOUR
LUCRATIVE PURPOSE

Often I have heard people—especially women—say that others are always coming to them with their problems. Many people describe this as a draining part of their lives, and wonder why it would be so negative if it were truly their purpose. Having others rely on you for constant help can sap a vital core energy you need to keep focused on yourself.

A true lucrative purpose is vitalizing, not draining. In this case, if it energizes you to help other people, great. However, if the way you are constantly giving to others is not energizing, you may need to put some limits on who you help and how you can help them.

Another stumbling block when people search for their lucrative purpose is that they often feel it must be a grand purpose in the world's eyes. A woman stood up at a recent talk I gave and said, "I want to be Mother Teresa or somebody." I so appreciated her honesty in expressing her feeling that if her calling or purpose were not grand or holy, it wasn't "right" or good enough, and, therefore, would not be fulfilling. I know so many people who want to do or be something huge to benefit humankind and then suffer a lack of personal fulfillment because they can't even take one small step toward this enormous goal.

"Remember," I told this woman, "Mother Teresa did not become Mother Teresa by anointing the masses all at once. She started with one sick man, whom she took home when no hospital would have him. She became a symbol of selfless caring by ministering to one person at a time. You don't have to save the world, just be *your* version of Mother Teresa, every day, to everyone you encounter. Start with yourself, and then your cat, and see where that takes you."

We all need to heed such advice, myself included.

The evolution of your lucrative purpose may land you somewhere grand, but it is not grand goals but simply living daily with your lucrative purpose in mind that will lead you in the end to fulfillment. If following your lucrative purpose leads to something huge, this will occur naturally—you won't have to force it. It will be the result of your true achievement: discovering your lucrative purpose.

THE DISCOVERY PROCESS

There are three steps to uncovering your lucrative purpose:

1. Recognizing who you are for other people—what purpose they see you fulfilling in their lives.
2. Dissecting the true meaning of your dreams and aspirations. Your long-held dreams may lead to a slightly different reality from what you might have expected.
3. Picking up the clues from your world that reflect these dreams and aspirations. Those who know and love you may hold the wisdom to point you to your lucrative purpose.

Let's look at each of these steps in turn. It may help you to think of them not as linear steps but as "access points," three different ways that may offer the key to unlocking your lucrative purpose. Explore each one to determine which speaks to you most clearly.

THE FIRST ACCESS POINT:
IT'S NOT WHAT YOU'VE DONE,
IT'S WHO YOU'VE BEEN

When trying to chart a course for our futures, we often resort to figuring out what we can do next by following the example of what we
have done in the past. We'll look at our résumé, training, degrees,
qualifications, or experience, and try to determine what work would
match our profile. The past is a good place to look for career inspiration, but I believe you're looking at the wrong part of the past.

Don't look at what you've done; look at who you've been.

- What have employers and coworkers come to rely on you for?
- What have the people in your life naturally come to you for?
- How have people used you? Who have you been for them?
- Have people come to you because they needed a listener or
  needed to solve a problem? Have people come to you to inspire
  creative ideas or model successful risk-taking?

Back when I was a waitress, my coworkers included aspiring talent of all kinds: other actors, rock singers, clothing designers, would-
be restaurateurs, fine artists, scholars, and so on. What we had in
common was that we were all stopping here only temporarily, as we
aimed for other things.

Invariably, at some time or another, every one of my colleagues
sat me down and asked me to help as each orchestrated plans to
achieve desired goals. Even then, I was always helping others see the
forest instead of the trees.

I always wondered: "Why me? Why do people ask me to help
when they are trying to reach a goal?" It's only in hindsight that I
understand that I was the guide for these people, someone who ushered them toward their desires. Even further back in my life, I had
been a resident's assistant in college and often did the same thing for
students. To all these people, I was not so much "fellow waitress,"

"aspiring actress," or even "enforcer of dormitory rules." They saw me as a guide to their goals and dreams. My natural path—my lucrative purpose—was being laid even then.

Marlo Morgan's *Mutant Message Down Under* describes an aboriginal tribe in the outback of Australia whose members are named not by a given name and a surname as Westerners traditionally use. Instead, people are designated by the function they serve in the tribe: memory keeper, peacemaker, cook, medicine man, kin to birds, female healer, the elder. Each person's role was who he or she was. A name changed only when the person developed a new role, and when that new purpose emerged, the individual celebrated a birthday. If we all honored and valued ourselves in this way, ours would be a very different world.

WISDOM STORY: MEET GREGORY
FROM WHAT YOU DO TO WHO YOU ARE

Gregory, who works in the biotech field, recently shared his story at a seminar of mine. Upon recognizing how people used him and how he got the most satisfaction out of his life and work, Gregory started telling people he was a master motivator. He stopped using his job title or any other label that described what he "did."

Just before making this discovery of his innate purpose, Gregory had become dissatisfied at his job and started looking for a new position. However, once he put his finger on his purpose, he pulled back the effort on his job search because he had a feeling that if he focused on this discovery, the perfect job would find *him*. (Smart guy!) Gregory altered the emphasis of his efforts at his current job so that what he did centered primarily around being a motivator of others.

One day, he went to an industry golf event. Asked by one of the players in his tournament what he did, he told the man he was a master motivator. As it turned out, his golf partner was the president of another company. This man was so impressed with the positive energy coming from Gregory that he offered him a chance at the perfect job before the round was over.

Gregory did indeed get the job doing more of what he loved for a lot more money than he was making before—all because he identified his lucrative purpose.

WISDOM WRITING

It's your turn to approach the first access point to your lucrative purpose. Think back over your life and see if you can find a common thread in how people have used you. Ask yourself:

- What have people always come to me for? Advice? A loan? A helping hand? Comforting?
- Who have I been for people? A truth-teller? A disciplinarian? A catalyst? An instigator?
- What role do I play most often: the teacher? the nurturer? the leader? the risk taker? the healer? the maverick? the motivator? the soother? the peacemaker?

Write your ideas down in your wisdom journal. Do any of your findings surprise you? Do you notice a consistent thread running through your past (people have pretty much always treated you the same), or have your roles changed? Has your lucrative purpose made itself known?

THE SECOND ACCESS POINT: THE ESSENCE OF THE DREAM

Dreams can be a window to the soul. But how many of us have had our dreams become our nightmares? We sometimes stop using our unfulfilled visions as a form of inspiration and use them instead as a bat to beat ourselves with. We see our unrequited dreams as a broken promise to ourselves, or a goodness that life has cheated us of.

Yes, for some of us the dream to be a teacher, business executive, or athlete was precisely the first step in pursuing and accomplishing the career goal. For others of us that dream was only a metaphor or a clue that we did not know how to decipher. Breaking that code is what I call discovering the essence of the dream. This is the second access point for uncovering your lucrative purpose.

Discovering the essence of the dream means uncovering the most tangible parts of your dreams, which usually have to do with how your dream serves others. For example, Victoria once told me of her dream of someday owning her own floral shop, where she could create unique and unusual designs. In real life, she had no desire to work for another florist. Her dream was having her own store. It was that or nothing.

When I asked Victoria to tell me the essence of her dream, she said it was to brighten people's lives through flowers and beauty. I pointed out that this was something she could do right then. She didn't need to wait for an elusive "someday" when she might have the financial resources to set up her own store. Understanding the essence of her dream allowed this woman to shift her focus from the store she didn't have. Instead, she began to seek ways she could fulfill the essence of her dream here and now. She did this by making a floral arrangement for a sick friend, who displayed the creation in her home. When her other friends came by they asked about the piece. These inquiries led to more business. Eventually, Victoria's reputation grew enough that a local florist asked her to work for him. Over time, it was obvious that she was responsible for a lot of their repeat business, so a partnership arrangement was made. In the end, she chose not to go off and start her own store. She enjoyed the partnership and camaraderie she had developed. By keeping her eyes on the essence of the dream, she achieved what she truly wanted. If she'd ignored the clues within the dream and focused only on its literal meaning, she would still be seeking true fulfillment today.

To Victoria's story, let me add my own experience to show you how much you can gain from understanding the essence of your dreams. In my twenties, I was desperately pursuing my dream to be a performer on Broadway. Up for a scholarship to an actor's program, I was asked at the final interview, "What is possible if you become successful as an actor?" My answer got me the scholarship: "If I succeed as an actor, it will mean that people saw a role I played that inspired them to change their life, or saw a scene where two characters worked out a difficult relationship, and were inspired to take action and do the same. And if I really succeed and become well-known and respected, I will be a voice for change."

It was only ten years later that the full impact of that question became evident. As I was struggling to find my direction in life, I remembered my answer and realized being a stage actor was only one form of how the essence of my dream could be expressed. Deep down, what I wanted was to have a positive impact on people's lives and help them make changes that would result in their happiness. It is no accident that the man who gave me that scholarship became my first coach several years later and ushered me into the profession that expresses the essence of my dream completely.

WISDOM IN ACTION

Finding the Essence of Your Dream

After attending one of my seminars, a woman wrote to me:

> For years I have struggled with not coming even close to living an unrequited passion of mine. I have always dreamed of conducting a choir or a symphony and it has plagued me that I have never done anything about it. My life has not afforded me that opportunity and I've gotten sidetracked tak-

ing care of reality. I have not even taken any steps toward it, so why do I suffer over it?

It was tonight, after hearing you speak, that I finally understood what that dream was trying to tell me. Being a conductor of music is bringing out the creative expression in people. This is something that I do in my current work and can find many avenues to do. Thank you, thank you for the freedom I now have. I don't have to feel depressed about this anymore. I am free!

Do you have an unfulfilled dream? Is there something that you aspire to now or did aspire to at one time? I'd like you to take a moment to write about your dream, if you have one, in your wisdom journal or computer file. Ask yourself the following questions:

- What is possible if you achieve, or had achieved, your dream? If you answer something like "I'd be rich" or "I'd be happy," then your reason is a creation from your head instead of your heart. Ignore it, and move deeper.
- How would other people benefit if you reached your dream?

Write down your answers and examine them closely. They may very well contain the true essence of your dream. You will know you have uncovered a clue as to what you are built to do when you latch on to something in your answers that:

- Is something you can start doing right away, such as, in my correspondent's example, helping others express themselves creatively.
- Is something that had to do with how your gifts relate to other people. The woman in the example saw that she was meant to nurture the talents of others.

If, through this exercise, you hit upon the essence of your dream, spend some time thinking about how this translates into your lucrative purpose. Record your thoughts in your journal.

What I want for you is that your dream no longer be a nightmare. If your answer to "What is possible if you achieve your dream?" does not have the two characteristics mentioned above, it will represent a more painful ride. If by doing the exercise you discovered that your dreams were more of a creation from your head instead of your heart ("I'd be rich," "I'd be happy," or "I'd be loved"), you may be experiencing a lot of stress and struggle due to the fact that these answers are all products of unmet needs—to be loved, or heard, or approved of, or taken care of. These needs surface and take hold because of what your childhood may not have provided. They will not prevent you from living your best life, but you'll need to make some adjustments to experience ease and to connect with your lucrative purpose. The next story shows you what I mean.

FINDING YOUR LUCRATIVE PURPOSE AMONG THE CHAOS OF UNMET NEEDS

Rachel was as grounded in the Doing aspect of life as anyone could be. She was driven and highly successful and had a great husband, a great house, the right cars, a successful social life, and all the trappings of success. But she started working with me because she had begun to recognize that her so-called success was taking a toll on her health and her personal life.

A highly rewarded and much applauded salesperson, Rachel had the dream of beating all the sales records at her company. Breaking many of them didn't seem to satisfy her, so I asked her to tell me what would be possible for her if she succeeded at her dream.

"I'd be on top," she answered. "I'd win. I'd beat everyone else." While this was the truth for her, it did not fit the criteria for finding her lucrative purpose. "Beating everyone else" was not something that could be put into effect immediately and it had nothing to do with serving other people. Rachel's unmet need to win more than anything else was like a starving monster; it was never satisfied with what it got and always wanted more. Rachel was on a treadmill of winning, being dissatisfied with her winning, and starting all over again.

Rachel went back to her first access point to explore finding her lucrative purpose and was dismayed by the recognition of whom she had been to other people on the job. Always competing, Rachel had been an antagonist to everyone she worked with. She realized the power she had to have an impact on people and that she was not making the kind of impact she wanted to be known for.

Financially and emotionally, Rachel was not in the position to leave her taxing job. However, she saw that in the meantime she could make her job easier by putting her energy toward finding and living her purpose instead of falling prey to the unmet needs that had been driving her. She reevaluated whom she wanted to be to other people and decided to have an impact on all those she met in a way that supported them, rather than taking from them, as she had done in the past.

This was Rachel's lucrative purpose. In working toward it at her current job, she so altered how she interacted with people that she was soon offered a new position, heading a team in a different department, and earned the same salary for working fewer hours with less stress.

Soon thereafter, Rachel discovered that she wanted to put her new people skills to work by becoming a coach and empowering others. She began her coach training with the same determination she had applied to using her lucrative purpose, and she now uses coaching daily in her work and her life.

■

By simply putting your purpose into action, luck will come and seemingly pluck you up and put you into a job or situation that best uses your gift. When you unlock the wisdom of your dream, your best life cannot help but find you. If you are in a work or life situation you hate, stop wasting your energy hating it and start being who you need to be to other people. Unlock the essence of whatever dream teases you today, and you will be released from that situation in time with little struggle from you. Change your focus and take action.

THE THIRD ACCESS POINT: THE PEOPLE AROUND YOU ARE THE REFLECTION OF YOUR PURPOSE

Throughout these pages, I've encouraged you to listen to yourself and ignore the assumptions and expectations of others. In the name of finding your lucrative purpose, this is one place where I am inviting you to listen to what others say. The final access point that could uncover your lucrative purpose is through the clues that may have been thrown into your path by other people.

We've already established that your true purpose is found by who you are to others and/or how the essence of your dream serves them. However, there is still more wisdom to be gleaned from those who know you and love you. Sometimes, when you are unable or unwilling to hear your own wisdom, your friends may be shouting it at you. Have you ever had several people tell you you would be well suited for the same specific career or trade? Well-meaning friends, relatives, colleagues, even strangers, are sometimes moved to make comments like "You should be a model" or "You'd make a great lawyer."

Often, we blow off such statements as trivial compliments, but perhaps we should learn to take heed. If you have been hearing the same theme over and over from different people, maybe it's time to pay attention. Others may not exactly be pointing out the perfect road for you, but what they are seeing may reflect a clue as to what would really bring you joy in life. For example, a teacher is someone who facilitates learning for others. If people have seen you as a potentially good teacher, this doesn't necessarily mean you're meant to be in front of a classroom. This could apply to whatever you are doing now, such as giving a presentation in your current job or mentoring your junior employees. It could be that you are supposed to merely raise the volume on using your teacherlike talents and see where that leads you.

Listening to others is another way of letting your world speak to you, instead of demanding answers all the time from your circumstances. The people around you are reflecting you. How they do so gives you yet another way of uncovering your lucrative purpose.

WISDOM IN ACTION

Take a moment to reflect on what people have said about you in the past in terms of what you "should be when you grow up." Were they right? Did you do what others thought you would? Do any of their comments still resonate with you as something you'd like to pursue? Was there a theme or underlying essence to all the suggestions?

Remember that the label or package on what other people envisioned you doing (teacher, lawyer, artist) might not be the exact clue you're supposed to pick up. Dissecting the *essence* of those labels could make a difference.

GO ON A QUEST

If your purpose has not jumped off these pages into your consciousness yet, take this challenge. Don't ask questions—just do it!

1. Talk to three to five people who know you well, either personally or professionally or both.
2. Ask them who they see you being to others and how they see you making a difference to people.
3. Listen. Do *not* interrupt. Just say thank you.

Now, do not question what they see. That is only your mind trying to get in the way. Write down their observations and consider them in your exploration.

WISDOM WRITING

Use your wisdom journal or computer file to creatively explore how you can put your lucrative purpose into action immediately. Without expecting an immediate outcome, write down five to ten specifics you can do to put your purpose into action. For example, once Rachel found her lucrative purpose, she resolved to put it into action by paying more attention to people than sales figures and by working on having more patience with everyone she came in contact with. To guide you to find these specifics, consider the following questions:

- How will you spend your time differently to express your purpose in both your job and your personal life?
- How will you behave differently with the people in your life?
- What must change today for you to live your lucrative purpose?

Take your specific action steps and start living your purpose now.

WRAPPING IT UP
WITH THE COACH

Discovering your lucrative purpose is vital to the Doing part of the process of connecting with the life blueprint, the one that is yours and yours alone. To uncover and stay in touch with your lucrative purpose, you'll want to remember the following:

- Ask yourself: How do people use me? What do people come to me for? Then do more of whatever it is.
- Dissect your dreams until you get to the essence of them. Put that essence into action right away.

- Listen to the messages about yourself that people are trying to get you to hear, and act on them.
- Go on a quest (p. 115).
- Live your purpose immediately, and observe how your life changes.

MAKE YOURSELF
A MAGNET

BECOMING A MAGNET
FOR YOUR BEST LIFE

According to *Merriam-Webster's Third International Dictionary,* a magnet is something that attracts. In this chapter, we will work on how to magnetize the field you inhabit so that you can attract "good" people, accomplishments, opportunities, and experiences into your life.

In the last chapter, we began to take the emphasis off of what you do and redirect it toward who you are. We began to look beyond your job or life description on paper to uncover your true lucrative purpose. As we saw, this purpose involves more than the dollars and cents in your life. It points you toward the most satisfying ways you can contribute to your world, whether in the context of raising your family or building a Fortune 500 company. In fact, attracting the work and purpose that leads to your best life is the first step toward becoming a magnet.

Although we are still talking about the Doing—that which we have to do to live our best life—after this chapter, we are crossing over into the Being part of the equation. Here, our Doing will revolve around what you have to *do* to *be* who you need to be. If you are confused by this, you won't be for long. I will walk you through it in this chapter.

The elements that make up your life—the people, your circumstances, your achievements, your sense of lucky breaks, and so on—can be termed the *what* of your life. Improving the quality of *who* we are starts to bring into our lives a higher quality of *what*. For instance, becoming someone who has more confidence could aid you in finding the perfect job instead of jumping at the first opportunity. You will have to take action to become more confident, but it is this action that will get you results and could become more important than conventional goal setting and follow-through.

What I am about to show you to is what I call the Power of Attraction. This concept was introduced to me by Thomas Leonard, a pioneer of personal coaching. The Power of Attraction challenges conventional wisdom, which says that positive results can occur only through linear and logical action, and instead takes a nonlinear approach. It asks you to work on yourself from the inside out to bring about the outcomes you want. Already, by making a simple contract and putting the focus of your activities on your lucrative purpose, you have begun this process. Here we will take it further, excavating your life blueprint even more. The Power of Attraction means that you will attract what you want to you, spending less time chasing your desires and success.

THE ENERGY EQUATION

The secret to attraction is to watch the energy equation in your life. The energy equation is based on the concept that everything you do either gives you energy or robs you of energy. Talking to some people may give you energy, talking to certain others might drain you. The way you deal with your financial life might enhance your life and energy, or it may be so consuming that it leaves you exhausted, with nothing to show for it. Your frame of mind about an issue could help you move forward, or it could drain you of the energy you need to tackle problems.

Becoming a magnet for your best life means your magnet (you) needs to be positively charged in order to attract. You must be engaged in relationships and activities that give you energy for your ability to attract to stay high. If not, your magnet (you) will repel. As you make yourself a magnet, you will monitor whether you are attracting or repelling in everything you do. The following box will help you distinguish the attitudes and behaviors of attraction from those of repulsion.

CHARACTERISTICS THAT MAKE YOU A MAGNET

Conditions That Attract	*Conditions That Repel*
Honoring your worth and time	Not honoring your worth and time
Expecting the best to happen	Worrying that the worst will happen
Doing your best	Cutting corners
Wanting everyone to succeed	Competing and wanting others to lose
Coming from your heart	Getting into power struggles
Maintaining integrity	Compromising values and ideals
Being aware and paying attention	Functioning on autopilot
Believing in abundance	Focusing on lack
Following your true desires	Forcing yourself to follow "have-to's"
Expressing gratitude and thanks	Feeling the world owes you
Enjoying the process	Valuing only the result or goal
Making clear agreements	Having unspoken or vague expectations

| Thinking how far you've come | Focusing on how far you have to go |
| Having clear intent and directed will | Having vague or undefined goals |

Whenever you allow something like one of the items in the "repel" column to impede the power of your magnet, your attention will be diverted from the good that awaits you. By taking care of everything that causes your magnet to repel, even if it's your own attitude, you create the opportunity for results to occur with less effort. Your power to attract is minimized by any chaos in your life, so it must go. That is why we made the simple contract. You are meant to have this magnetic ability, just as you are meant to be wired for wisdom. This is innate, but no one gave you a manual on how to use it, so you are learning that now.

If you are attracting great opportunities, you'll know it. Keep in mind that when things are going smoothly, energy is flowing; when things are bumpier, energy is spent in unproductive ways. When you notice this happening in your life, you'll know this is the time to stop what you're doing and investigate. Figure out what needs to be cleared up to allow the energy to flow again. The greater the energy flow, the higher your Power to Attract, and the clearer your life blueprint.

Your energy may be stuck for a variety of reasons—for instance, because you are struggling with something instead of getting help, because you have been hiding the truth about something (even from yourself!), or because you still have some Reckoning to do with your own mind.

A friend once handed me a Chinese finger trap, a woven bamboo cylinder about the size of a penny roll, asking that I insert my index fingers into either end. She then asked me to try to get my fingers out. My natural instinct was to pull hard from both ends. The cylinder tightened around my fingers. After many tries, it was clear that the only way out of the cylinder was to relax both fingers into it and gently ease each finger out.

The energy equation is similar. If something is stuck, the harder you fight with it, the harder it is to "unstick" it, to solve it. You waste energy by resisting or fighting, and you gain energy by conserving it for the action that will make a difference. The less you resist the problem, the easier it is to invite a solution.

RAISE THE CONDUCTIVITY OF YOUR LIFE

Let's focus now on four specific things you can do to increase the attraction quotient of your magnetism. Each embodies elements from the chart on pages 120–21, but they also include some new insights into what will make your magnet more attractive. Furthermore, you'll notice they all focus on who you have to be.

Be a Model

No, I'm not suggesting here that you become a fashion model. However, what you'll need to strive for to benefit from the ease of attraction is to demonstrate ideals that other people wish to emulate. By being someone whom people want to model part of themselves after, you'll find people drawn to you. This puts you in the position of meeting up with more opportunities. Being a model requires you and your life to be in great shape. By now, I hope, we've put you on that path via your simple contract.

Demonstrate Ease

It gives people great comfort to be in the presence of someone who is even tempered and who seems to be sailing through life. It also inspires them. The energy is flowing evenly and attraction can occur. Demonstrate an ease with yourself, and positive magnetism will flow your way.

Be Somebody

Of course, all of us are literally somebody, but *being somebody* means treating yourself with a level of respect so that others will not dare trespass upon you or your territory. In addition, being somebody makes you very attractive to others and raises your magnet's conductivity. People want to be in the positive aura of a person who is confident in and of themselves.

Show You Care

As long as you are not overextending yourself, putting other people ahead of your own agenda is hugely effective in creating positive energy in your life. As I've said before, people are the vehicle by which success will come to you, so it does make sense to invest in others. You will see that your attraction quotient will go up as you do so.

What Is Your Attraction Quotient?

Take this quiz to test your attraction quotient. It examines the four methods to increase your positive conductivity, measuring which ones could use improvement and attention right now on your way to attracting your best life.

Put a checkmark next to each item that accurately reflects how you are living right now.

Be a Model
____ I set and live up to standards I truly want.
____ I do not promise more than I can deliver.
____ I put my integrity above all else.
____ I have extensive boundaries that keep other people's problems at bay.

Demonstrate Ease
____ I do not suffer or struggle.
____ I don't complain.
____ I ask plainly for what I need.
____ I don't react to problems.

_____ I have more than enough of everything I need to live well.
_____ I accept the bad with the good about myself.

_____ I am solution oriented.
_____ I am grateful for what I have, regardless of whether it is enough

Be Somebody

_____ I do not make excuses.
_____ I admit when I am wrong.
_____ I have a strong circle of
_____ friends who support me.
_____ I am motivated internally, not externally.
_____ I invest in myself and my growth.
_____ I am in all my relationships by choice, not by obligation.
_____ I take responsibility for all my problems and concerns.

Show You Care

_____ I put people ahead of results.
_____ I don't just tell people I care— I show it.
_____ I give people the credit and acknowledgment they deserve.
_____ I can see faults in people and be compassionate and patient.
_____ I am more interested in what others have to say than in being the center of attention.
_____ I don't BS people, but I speak to them in a way that makes them feel good about themselves.

Count the number of checkmarks you made. Your total is your attraction quotient. Here's what your score means.

0–6 Thanks for being honest. You're probably low on energy and have more than your share of problems. Now you know what to work on.

7–13 Your magnet is still repelling quite a bit. Life could be easier, but you may now see what you need to do.

14–20 Good for you. Your magnet is attracting. You're probably feeling good and that is reflecting in your environment.

21–25 Congratulations! You're a magnet for the people and conditions you want for your life. Keep up the good work.

Did some of the items from the quiz jar you a bit? Is the entire notion of their being something to aspire to a foreign concept to you? If so, you are experiencing the shifts that occur when you start framing your world from a whole different set of criteria than before. If you are or were very externally referenced, measuring your happiness and success by others' approval and your material desires only, you will feel a little disoriented as you become internally referenced and start focusing on who you are being as a way to improve your life.

If you scored poorly and would like to do better, study the rest of this chapter extremely carefully. It will help you attain more conductivity. After you've digested the material and put it into effect, you may want to take the quiz again and see how your score has changed.

REDUCING YOUR IMPORTANCE INCREASES YOUR MAGNETISM

In *The Art of Dreaming*, Carlos Castaneda says that "most of our energy goes to upholding our importance." It is our ego that upholds our importance and will often get in the way of attracting our best life. It is therefore essential to the conductivity of our magnet that we reduce our ego and its importance. I often call the work of a coach "ego reduction therapy." An effective coach knows he has to keep in check his own ego's need to have the answers and be right, in order to tap the wisdom and answers the client already has.

When you decide to reduce your ego (the part of you that is full of fight and always wanting to feel justified and be right), you begin to expand your self, your wisdom, and the memory of your soul— who you are, in essence. The goal here is to bring these inner qualities to your outer material world and refrain from constantly trying to massage your ego with affirmations of how important you are. If you can do this, you will produce changes in your life in a gentler, more low-impact way.

Granted, if your job puts you in the middle of a dog-eat-dog field *and* you want to stay firmly in that world, reducing your importance will be a very difficult thing to do. However, ego reduction helps bring about results in an unconventional way. It may take a little longer to get results, but trust me, your investment in the process will be worth it. You already have the innate ability to attract results this way, if only your self-importance would let you believe that was enough.

One of my first experiences with ego reduction will illustrate how this concept can be surprisingly effective in increasing your power to attract. Soon after I gave up acting for good, an invitation arrived for a party given by my college alumni association. I decided to go, wearing the first business suit I'd ever bought, which I thought of as my "I am in business now" costume.

Since I had never been to an alumni event, I was nervous about how I should behave and what I should say. I was not yet used to my new identity of "businesswoman" and scared of networking, so I decided to use the magnet theory. I would say nothing, avoid schmoozing, and see if I could attract people to me by being a magnet.

Once I was at the party, although my mind and ego were screaming that I should *do* something, I stood in the middle of the room and made eye contact only with whoever wanted to. At different times, several people stopped by to ask who I was and what I did. By the end of the evening I had business cards from three potential clients. I remember one of them in particular, a woman who said, "There's something about your energy. I don't know, but I was just drawn to talk to you."

Our need to uphold our importance forces us to feel as if we have to impress or take action in order to have an impact. I hope my example helps you see how *who we are* can in itself be enough.

WISDOM IN ACTION

Return to the "What Is Your Attraction Quotient" quiz and choose an item from the "Demonstrate Ease" or "Show You Care" section that would help you reduce your ego/importance. Put the item into action for the next twenty-four hours and record your impressions in your wisdom journal. For example, if you chose "I am more interested in what others have to say than being the center of attention," from the "Show You Care" section, you could spend the next twenty-four hours being a much more attentive listener—asking more questions and being curious—and then record in your journal what that did to your ego and how you felt. Was it hard? Did you have to struggle to pay attention? What was the benefit? What about this experience is worth repeating and making a part of who you are?

YOUR ENERGY EXCHANGES AND CONDUCTIVITY

It's one thing to sit in a room and imagine attracting results or to do as I did at that cocktail party; however, these aren't the activities we normally fill our days with. The way to apply this to everyday life is to keep an eye on the energy exchanges in your life.

Energy exchanges occur in many ways: between you and other people, between you and your money, between you and your job. Granted, these criteria for judging your day and activities will probably be quite different from what you are used to, but measuring your success in energy can help you understand why you may not be living the life you want. As we said earlier, everything you have and do will either give you energy or rob it from you. The energy will either get stuck or flow. When it's stuck, we experience frustration; when it flows, we flourish. When we are stuck and our energy is being drained, our conductivity (the ability to attract) is low and we are not at our best. When the energy flows, our best self can reign, our conductivity is high, and we can be a magnet.

To monitor the energy exchanges in your life, detect the places where you need to stop doing so much and start making adjustments to who you are being. In other words, you have to observe how you are acting in the situation. This strategy, however, will work best when you have taken responsibility for your life and taken action as we discussed in implementing the simple contract in chapter 5.

For example, a client named Kelly was always very nervous about her finances, despite the fact that she was doing all the right things—saving while paying down her debt, following a budget, investing wisely, and so on. Nevertheless, she never felt financially secure, no matter how much money she was making or how well her investments were doing. Her lack of comfort with her finances was a huge energy drain in her life.

Kelly compared her situation with her friend Elizabeth, who had been in the same boat financially when they met. Over the years, Elizabeth had made a lot of money, saved wisely, and led a prosperous lifestyle, even though she hardly cared at all about the specifics of her financial condition, such as the yield on her investments. Kelly was frustrated that her efforts to manage her money did not pay off in the same ways things had for Elizabeth.

It was clear to me that my client was taking the same responsible actions as her friend, so I asked Kelly one day, "What does Elizabeth do that you don't?"

"She doesn't worry, complain, or constantly obsess about it," she answered.

That was exactly the point.

Kelly used some of the suggestions in chapter 3 to gain perspective, and her magnet's conductivity increased. Within six months she reported feeling "richer." The numbers reflected that, as well as her state of mind.

So, who do you have to be to have an even energy exchange with your money? with your family? your friends? your coworkers? your life? Can you distinguish between what consumes your life's energy and what enhances it? The dead giveaway is your energy level. What is increasing it and what is robbing energy from you?

WISDOM IN ACTION

Go on an energy watch for twelve waking hours. During this time, pay very close attention to every activity and person you encounter and monitor your energy level.

Did the task, conversation, or meal add to your level of energy or take away from it? When you spoke with people, did you feel energized or drained? Where applicable, who were you being in these situations? Were you part of the problem or the solution? Were you draining your own energy with your attitude or anxiety, or were you drained by the other person or by what they were doing?

Record each thing you notice and see where the energy "vampires" are in your life. These could be other people, certain activities, or even you yourself—that is, your own choices about where to invest your energy.

Also, please keep in mind that adrenaline, coffee, sugar, or any other rush-producing substance does not count as an energy enhancer. The energy boost these things provide is not sustainable; therefore, it ends up being more of a drain than an enhancer.

WISDOM STORY: MEET JUDY

INCREASING YOUR CONDUCTIVITY BY CORRECTING THE ENERGY EXCHANGE

Judy, a mother of two and a part-time insurance broker, had come to coaching to get the most out of her business. As we worked on her business strategies, we also examined the rest of her life. For instance, Judy complained about always feeling tired and she had frequent colds and sinus infections.

Judy's mother, who called her about three times a day, claimed to not be able to make a decision without her daughter's assistance. Ever since she was widowed, she had relied heavily on Judy. Judy felt taking care of her mother was her duty.

When Judy did the energy watch exercise, much to her dismay, her mother came up as one of the biggest energy drains in her life. Although this was hard to acknowledge, it was undeniable that her mother's dependence, as well as her hypercritical nature, had become a very heavy burden.

In hitting upon this discovery, it became clear to Judy why she always felt worn out.

Nonetheless, Judy was terrified at the thought of having to correct the situation. Like most people would, she thought any possible way to do so would devastate her mother. Then she was laid low for three weeks with the flu. Lying in bed with barely enough energy to lift her head, she worked out in her mind what she could tell her mother to correct the energy exchange between them and increase her own positive magnetism.

As her mother telephoned with her daily appeals for help and direction, Judy began responding by saying things like "What do *you* think, Mom?," "What are *you* going to do, Mom?," and "I know you've been used to me doing everything for you, but I am going to be a little more selfish with my time these days, so I hope you'll also ask your other kids to help too." These were difficult things for Judy to say, but she was patient and persistent and she held her resolve when her mother felt threatened or lost her temper.

Once her mother got over the initial shock of the rules changing, there was a huge, positive difference in their relationship. It became a more loving one, and Judy stopped resenting her mother and was much more helpful in kinder, more profound ways. She felt more energized by their exchanges and over time, had fewer colds. And her business increased by 20 percent, because she had more time and energy to focus on what mattered there. By correcting this energy exchange with her mother, this daughter even increased her income.

TOO MUCH OF A GOOD THING

By watching the energy exchanges in your life, you are managing the quality of your life and have gone a level deeper in excavating your life blueprint. You attract results instead of chasing them. As you become more and more "attractive," you'll have to watch out for the one danger in all this.

The fact is you can be too attractive and too magnetic if you don't know how to control the magnetism. When you are attracting people at an astounding rate, there may be more people and opportunities than you can reasonably take advantage of without exhausting yourself. When you become a viable magnet, other people can't even articulate why they want to be in your company—they are just drawn to you. All this attention can be too much for anyone. It is too easy to fall prey to wanting to meet all the needs of these outside influences.

What to do—or should I say, who to be? Be someone who is clear on what their criteria is for what they allow into their life. As harsh as it may sound, it will become essential for you to continually monitor the quality of who and what comes into your life. As you excavate the "higher-quality" you, you'll have to become clearer and clearer about who and what keeps your energy high. You may find that some of the aspects of your life that were okay before have begun to drain you. Therefore, you'll need new criteria for your life. As you attract more and more people and opportunities, you'll need some measure to weed through it all. The next section will help.

UNCOVERING THE OBSTACLES TO YOUR CONDUCTIVITY

If you are still adjusting to the idea of looking at your life in terms of energy and magnetism, it might help to realize that the common denominator is recognizing what is and is not acceptable to you in your life. Our work is leading you toward that recognition, so that problems can be kept to a minimum and your conductivity can be restored and then enhanced. As you decide more and more quickly what can stay in your life and what must go, you will get better at learning to say no. You will be able to distinguish between attracting gold and attracting lint, and you will communicate it in a way that keeps your energy level high without lowering the energy of anyone around you.

Being able to identify what is acceptable to you and what is not can sound trivial, but most of us allow so much more to happen to us and around us than we have to. This can take the form of the "deer in the headlights" effect, where you don't even know you were hit until after it's over. I also call it getting slimed (as in *Ghostbusters*): someone does something completely inappropriate to you (for instance, raising her voice, making a rude remark, acting in a threatening manner) and you just stand there taking it, in stunned perplexity.

For a person, action, remark, or event to be unacceptable, it doesn't even have to be blatantly wrong. It could just be something that does not fit with what you want for your life or that makes you uncomfortable. What it does do is take energy from you and lower your magnet's ability to attract, by taking time, energy, and attention away from what matters to you.

For example, it may be unacceptable that your neighbors are cold and unresponsive. You could be cold right back, or you could try to extend yourself to them in an effort to get to know them. Imagine that after several attempts to get closer to your neighbors, the situation remains unchanged. Knowing that you tried and letting it go may be exactly what it takes to make the situation okay again for you. Making something acceptable doesn't necessarily mean you have to fix or solve it; sometimes, you merely have to make peace with it. Reconciling something like this for yourself allows the energy to flow again, which allows your magnetism to increase its intensity. In order to do that, you are asking yourself to stretch who you are being in the situation. You have to decide who you want to be about this instance versus what you want to do. The result is peace of mind and permission to return to your best life.

WISDOM STORY: MEET KARL

HOW TO ASSERT WHAT IS UNACCEPTABLE WITHOUT HURTING OTHERS

Karl was a designer at a desktop publishing firm who came to me for coaching. He was an efficient worker, often getting his assignments done early. Whenever that happened, he would then create some of his own graphic designs on the job. No one seemed to mind—in fact, his extra work inspired a lot of the folks who shared his office. One woman, Trina, frequently stopped at his desk to see what he was working on. In the most innocent way, she would ask if she could use one of his ideas or base a project of hers on something she'd seen him do. He couldn't think of a good enough reason to say no, so he let her.

As Karl and I were discussing how he could become a magnet for opportunity and some of the areas of his life that were acceptable and unacceptable, his work environment came up for examination. All of a sudden, Karl started getting angry. He could barely contain himself as he shouted: "It is completely unacceptable to me that my office mates use my ideas!" He'd been bottling up these feelings for so long that it felt great to voice them aloud.

Karl realized that he was annoyed because of both his protective feelings toward his own work and his frustration with Trina for not recognizing her own ample talents. As we looked at ways to communicate his feelings to Trina, he decided that he would no longer give her his work; instead, he would encourage her to come up with her own ideas and offer her some assistance.

This is how he phrased it: "Trina, it's unacceptable to me that you don't see that you can come up with good ideas too. It's not okay for you to look at my work anymore. Let me know how else I can help you come up with some of your own."

Giving everything doesn't make you a magnet—it simply leaves you drained. On the other hand, when you give out information about your boundaries and what you are willing to do, your magnetism is left intact and can even help others much more than you may think. Karl set a very clear boundary about what actions were and were not permitted, thus making his position known to Trina without hurting her. Although at first she didn't appreciate the challenge, once she came up with some great ideas on her own, she saw how his policy was ultimately better for her. The most productive way to say no is not to tear the other person down, but to work to build her up. Doing this will increase your magnetism.

WISDOM IN ACTION

The next time you have to say no to something you had once thought acceptable, follow these steps to do so in a productive way:

1. Determine what is unacceptable.
2. Take responsibility, for what is unacceptable; don't make it the other party's fault.
3. State specifically what is not okay with you.
4. Ask for the change(s) you'd like to see.
5. When appropriate, offer support in a new way.

IDENTIFYING THE IDEAL

So far in this chapter, we've explored the conditions that repel and attract, the impact of energy exchanges on your life, and how the unacceptable can be an obstacle to your ultimate conductivity. It's now time to examine what will fuel your magnetic ability the most: identifying the ideal for every part of your life. When you explore what is ideal, what you *really* want, you can accelerate the rate at which you attract results.

The ideal is the best-case scenario, the dream, the wish, the best circumstance you can imagine. The ideal is an inspiring vision and direction motivated from within. Your ideal doesn't have to be heady or grandiose either. It can be used in everyday, practical terms. For example, what is your ideal work schedule, who is your ideal baby sitter, what is your ideal job description, or who is your ideal lawyer or bookkeeper?

Notice I did not use the word "perfect," which is not the same thing as "ideal." Perfection tends to be rigid. When we look for the ideal, we may have perfection as a goal but we retain enough flexibility to find something different, perhaps even better, that we may not have anticipated. In my opinion, being a perfectionist is the ultimate lack of self-acceptance, in that we need the outside world to reflect perfection so that we can know we are okay. That is why perfectionism can be so rigid and so damaging and why the search for perfection will repel instead of attract.

The ideal attracts because it's meant to be a receptacle to contain your dream. Think of it like a pitcher holding water. If we don't allow the water to be kept in a container, it could run off, dry up, disperse, or evaporate. Similarly, without something to catch them, our dreams for ourselves can disappear or we can lose track of them. When you hold the vision of an ideal scenario for some part of your life, you have created criteria by which to measure your present circumstances and those that show up as you work toward living your best life.

Sometimes we have an ideal situation in mind and we will surpass that ideal. Other times, what we thought was ideal is not so when we attain it. Regardless, having the picture allows you to follow your own wisdom.

WISDOM WRITING

For each area of your life (relationships, career/work, money, health and well-being, physical environment) or anything else you are looking to improve or create:

1. Write down and describe what the ideal scenario looks like. If you could have what you truly wanted for this part of your life, what would it be? Be specific, and resist the temptation to edit yourself. For example, if your ideal job is in a firm with people you look forward to seeing every morning, where you are able to double your current salary, and you have to only do the part of your job that you love—say, talking to clients—then write that down.

2. Write down and describe what's real and true about this part of your life now. What is missing? What are your complaints?

3. If you are not yet living your ideal scenario, write down five steps (or as many you need) that could connect the real with the ideal. (Use the highlighted action points from the Wisdom Writing exercise on page 000 to help you.)

4. Once you've written the ideal scenarios for as many parts of your life as you would like to improve, you must take action. Only action can make it real. Get the support you need to prod you, help you, or cheer you on. And remember, use your written ideal scenario as the measuring stick for what you allow in your life. It's okay to say no to some person or situation that does not fit the ideal. It takes courage to be able to trust that by saying no you are leaving room for the yes (the ideal) to show up.

BEING SPECIFIC

In this part of the book, you are letting who you really are shine through, and if you've improved your life's infrastructure by delivering on the simple contract, you are ready for bigger things. That is why we are spending time on "the ideal." You may find that the desires and action you described in the Wisdom Writing above were more radical or have helped you expect more for yourself than anything you wrote in your simple contract.

Earlier, we had to let our life tell us what is needed from us. Once we have done that and made the foundation solid, we can turn the tables once again, and start asking more from our life and ourselves. Not in the painful ways in which we might have done before we read this far, but in a way that does not allow us to lose. By the time you reach this stage of excavating your blueprint, your life should be in good enough shape that even if you do not reach the ideal, you've lost nothing. When the consolation prize is already pretty terrific, going for the ideal becomes a painless gamble. And ironically, when we can have that freedom to pursue the ideal with ease and detachment, it is more likely that we can achieve it. That said, the final key to attracting the ideal is being specific.

As you saw in one of the items from the chart on pages 120–21 called "Characteristics That Make You a Magnet," being specific is important to your ability to attract. Furthermore, being specific even if what you want seems out of your league may be just the energy your magnet needs to bring the "improbable" thing to you. When you can name it, you can claim it. The next story illustrates what I mean.

WISDOM STORY: MEET CHRISSIE

ATTRACTING THE IDEAL BY GETTING MORE SPECIFIC

Once her son turned two, Chrissie wanted to return to work and set about finding the right day-care situation. After checking out the best centers in the area, she was very frustrated and unhappy with what was available. She wondered if she was being too picky as the start date for her job loomed.

I asked Chrissie to write a profile of her ideal day-care provider. As she listed the situation she wanted for her son and the kind of activities and people she wanted him to be with, she realized she had been barking up the wrong tree. She had thought a center was the best choice she could make as a parent and yet the ideal profile she had written more accurately described a private-care situation. However, Chrissie was afraid she could not afford this pricier option, so I asked her to include the ideal price in her profile.

During the next two weeks, Chrissie kept her written profile with her, asked friends, put an ad in the paper, and was overwhelmed with responses. She soon found someone who fit most, if not all, of the criteria, including the price. The ideal profile had helped her attract what she wanted very quickly. Its clearness and specificity had been important elements in experiencing attraction and becoming a magnet.

■

Any problem you're confronted with is also an opportunity to grow, to choose wisely and to do your best. It is a chance to gain new skills that will become a permanent part of who you are. It is how we grow through these situations that determines our wisdom. If we face the lesson and grow through it, we are wiser. If we resist, avoid, or otherwise delay our growth, we keep the wisdom at bay. We choose to lead a more difficult life. One of my mentors says, "As magnets, we attract who and what we are ready for; the only way to attract better is to grow, grow, grow."

WRAPPING IT UP WITH THE COACH

As we leave the Doing portion of this book, you have the tools and insights you need to be responsible for your life and start enjoying the benefits of the journey you've undertaken. Making yourself a magnet will be invaluable as you move from the work of the doing to reaping the rewards of being. As you work on living your best life, a fulfilling one that is not a struggle to sustain, remember these points to raise the conductivity of your magnet:

- Concentrate on who you are being, not what you are doing.
- Raise your conductivity by being a model, demonstrating ease, being somebody, and showing you care.
- Watch your energy exchanges.
- Know what is unacceptable for you and communicate boundaries.
- Dream big and deal with the ideal.
- Be specific.
- Take action and grow, grow, grow!

PART THREE

THE BEING

A S YOU PROGRESS THROUGH THE THREE STAGES OF EXCA-
vating your life's blueprint, your degree of consciousness will
increase, although you may not be aware of it. By now, you
should have evidence that your wisdom wiring is reliable.

Your new level of awareness is what will allow things to happen
more quickly. You will not need as much energy, nor will it take so
much effort to manage your life or to make new things happen. You
will be making different choices, which will require less repetition of
old patterns that used to cause you pain. You won't have to repeat the
same mistakes over and over before you "learn your lesson." In fact,
it will seem as if you won't have as many hard lessons to learn. All this
will help good things happen in your life more quickly.

In your new state of being, you'll find that it doesn't take as much
knowledge to feel secure and move forward in your life. Your knowledge is there. Your wisdom is there. You can feel confident about this.
If you don't, go back and review your weak points in the strategies
we've covered so far.

In the stage of Being, you will be starting to trust yourself more
and you'll be able to take action based solely on what you feel is right.
You'll have stopped relying solely on doing as the only confirmation of
your worth and existence, so you'll be free to move through life with
more ease, being more comfortable with who you are.

In this section, we are going to let go. We have finished the self-
evaluation that comes with reckoning and the rethinking, exploring,
and fixing that comes with doing. We've taken action in so many
parts of our lives. Now finally, we are going into the free fall—the Being. After all, as Thomas Leonard has often said, we are human *beings,* not human *doings.* It is essential to become comfortable with
being, the place where we relinquish effort and control and still expect a great outcome. Without this Being section, we would not be
complete. Here, we will tap into the resources of your spirit to put
the final touches on your excavation of your life blueprint.

For the purpose of this section, let's define spirituality as the belief that there is some kind of unspoken universal connection among
all humankind. The specifics of that belief—whether in God, angels

and spirit guides, the self (and only the self), or some other type of entity—doesn't matter. All that matters is that you are willing to explore tapping into that collective consciousness for your own benefit and that of others—that you consider that there is a reserve of untapped information out there that can facilitate the unfolding of the life you are meant to live.

It does not matter what your religious persuasion is—or even if you have one—because I will not interfere with the tenets of your belief system. I may, however, be asking you to stretch beyond your comfort zone to explore new parts of yourself. By now, you should know this goes with the program.

Without veering from the practical approach we have taken so far, we will delve into three areas that will encourage you to trust that your life is on autopilot toward the best version of itself. Mastering silence, harnessing your intuition, and giving up the need to know are the tools needed to draft the final pieces of your blueprint. In my opinion, this is the most fun.

———

BECOME A MASTER
AT FOCUSING

———

MASTERING FOCUS MAY SOUND LIKE AN ACTION-ORIENTED activity, but nothing could be further from the truth. Mastering focus depends on becoming still, something that defies most conventional wisdom on how to get what you want from life. You may say, "Ah, more duality," but nothing is a better partner to taking action than being still. Stillness allows the most effective action to emerge, helping to settle the chaos and uncover the action and direction that will do the most good.

You might wonder why this book did not start with this section, since it reveals the most wisdom about our lives. Quite simply, you would not have been ready for this. The work we have done up to now has cleared the way to being able to master focus.

In this chapter, we will explore three ways of mastering focus:

1. Focusing through silence.
2. Focusing through intention.
3. Focusing on your own life, not on the lives of others.

These three elements pack a mean punch when it comes to having an impact on the quality of your life. Once the other pieces we have described in the previous strategies are in place, these elements of focus can really be effective in creating results with seemingly little effort.

SILENCE IS THE NATURAL ORGANIZER

In our harried and hassled world, the last thing we may feel we have time for is finding a few moments of quiet in each day. When I first recommend silence as an exercise to my clients, some resist the idea or, at best, try to implement it incredulously. Almost invariably, they soon discover the benefits to be found in making the time to be still.

Over time, several important things happen in silence. Self-criticism ceases. The thought process becomes more orderly. True values emerge, and your own priorities come to the forefront and take precedence over those of the day's schedule and the world around you. Any decision you come to in silence is based on strength.

Practicing silence allows for clarity and order to emerge. Its cumulative effect adds up to less reliance on schedules and to-do lists and more understanding of the natural priority and order of things. When you become comfortable with silence, you invite a natural organization to your life that doesn't require as much of your effort and control. Practicing silence also increases the power of your ability to do the things that will make a real difference in your day, which I call your hit list. Many of my clients have reported that as they learned to be still, they would seem to get their work done more quickly and even find themselves with extra time to get ready for the next day.

Most of the time, the things we do require only one side (right or left) of our brain. Practicing silence yields a higher output of organization, clarity, and calm because it causes the two hemispheres of our brain to work together at the same time. The alpha state that this creates allows for the broader scope of awareness and the tapping our full potential. In that relaxed state lies the greatest pool of your innate wisdom. The more we go into this state the easier it is for the brain to produce this state on its own. That is why it gets easier with practice and why it has a cumulative effect. I will walk you through several ways to practice silence in this chapter.

In order to effectively allow silence to be our natural organizer, we need to be comfortable *with* silence and be comfortable *in* it. So often, silence makes us feel uncomfortable. It does that because it asks us to grow. We have to grow to accommodate what we face in that silent space. Most of us would rather have dental surgery than feel the discomfort of battling with ourselves. Silence allows the truth to be revealed. It allows you to willingly give up your illusions in favor of this truth. In silence, you will be able to hear and see the real you and the priorities that will best express you.

Silence is that suspended moment when life holds its breath to allow you to catch yours. Silence is intimacy. The silences in a conversation are those places where the words stop and the souls can meet. We all long for these quiet places, we even crave them, but many of us are terrified to visit them. We keep talking. We forget to breathe. We fill our lives with endless activities to avoid touching the inner core that silence unveils.

You may have noticed that I haven't used the word "meditation." Many people find that word intimidating. People feel they must know how to meditate before trying to embrace silence as a daily practice in their life. However, although practicing silence *is* meditation, there is not one set way to do it. For instance, I was never formally taught any meditative techniques, but for years I have succeeded at quieting my mind. I still have no idea whether I meditate or not.

I am about to show you different ways to practice silence, and you may come up with a few of your own. The one requirement is that you find time to be quiet every day. Practicing silence daily is necessary if you're going to learn to cultivate the awareness and higher state of mind it can provide. How you choose to practice silence is up to you, as long as you achieve the goal of quiet contemplation, probably the one principle all spiritual and religious practices hold in common.

Mastering silence comes with its obstacles. You can expect both your mind and your body to fidget. If you are very new to the practice of sitting still in silence, you may be tempted to give up immediately. Try to do as well as you can, keeping in mind that finding silence and being still does not need to be done perfectly. Soon you'll find your mind and body adjusting more readily to times of silence.

You may want to practice thinking of silence as plugging into an energy source. Imagine recharging the battery in your cell phone. It's best to recharge it fully, but even if you can only charge it for a few minutes, the phone will run longer.

Choosing the time to be silent is your first step. The morning, just after rising, and just before bed at night are good times. These times are already filled with rituals, and times of silence can easily become a new, valued ritual. However, you may choose to be silent at some point during the day. Some people use their office, others find time for silence just before gearing up to do the biggest task of the day. If you are home with kids, it can be harder—but I often find that inviting my three year old to join me allows me to avoid being distracted and models quiet time for him.

Where you find your time for silence is your choice, but it will need to be a time that you can count on keeping with yourself. As you get used to how you feel when you become silent, you'll find you can enter that centered place almost instantly anywhere you may be, whether waiting in line at the bank, sitting in a theater waiting for a movie to start, on a subway or train, or even while enduring an endless meeting at the office. The more you practice, the more the positive influences of silence can be yours anywhere.

The most important part of focusing on silence is knowing that facing yourself in the silence will generate more and more rewards in time.

WISDOM STORY: MEET BILL

MEETING YOURSELF IN THE SILENCE

Bill had recently been promoted to a management position in a large international recruiting firm that specialized in information technology. Feeling even more pressure to perform well, he hired me as his coach to help him become a better manager. In a five-week crash course, we improved his communication style, his organization and delegation skills, and his relationship building. Once his main concerns were taken care of, I wanted us to get down to the real work Bill had in front of him.

As I do with most clients, I asked Bill to start making room in his life for fifteen minutes of silence a day. When he found this incredibly difficult, we reduced the time to five minutes, but even that didn't work. We looked at what made spending five minutes in silence so hard for him, and found that while Bill had lived by himself for some time, he had developed habits to keep from ever really being alone *with* himself. He kept the TV or radio on as background noise; he smoked; he drank wine in the evening. In sum, anything to avoid confronting himself in the silence.

Although Bill repeatedly asked to put quitting smoking in his simple contract, I would not let him. To my mind, such a specific "giving up" goal would have been a distraction to the real work of learning to be still and discovering himself in the silence created. At my recommendation, Bill started by changing his focus on the brisk walk he took with his dog every morning. Instead of looking at the homes and cars on their route, he began to take deeper breaths and to concentrate on the trees and the birds as he walked. Soon, he was ready to sit still for three to five minutes daily. He learned to focus on his breathing and, after practicing some of the techniques you will learn in this chapter, he began to turn off his 100-mile-per-hour mind and dwell in the real mental quiet that his silent time made possible.

During the summer, Bill took a hiatus from our coaching, enjoying his time with extended family at the beach on the weekends and working a slower week. When he came back in the fall, he announced with pride that he had quit smoking and drinking! I asked what changed, and he replied, "One day, I just woke up and realized I was trying to kill myself with this stuff. I didn't need to do that anymore."

In the silence, Bill got in touch with the part of himself who really did want to live fully, and he was thus able to be powerful in a new way. I had known that the only way he would quit his bad habits was by addressing them at this soul level. He had been afraid to connect with himself, but once he did, he found the opening for so much more: his health, a sense of mental well-being, new interests in old passions, and even a satisfying romantic relationship.

THE METHOD TO THE SILENCE

Now that I've told you what practicing silence can do for you, it's time to get down to the specifics of how you can reach this state.

The Proper Place and Time

Find a comfortable place to take your silent time. You might create a special place in your home devoted to this activity. It could be a chair or a place where you are comfortable on the floor. You might want to sit on a pillow. Make sure you are comfortable, because it will interfere with your ability to focus if you are not. But don't lie down.

You might ask, if you are going to meditate first thing in the morning or last thing at night, why not do it lying down? You're already in bed, right? The reason is that you are too likely to fall asleep and the brain activity of sleep is different from practicing silence. You need to be conscious, yet in a suspended state of higher awareness. Lying down won't cut it. Neither will browsing through a magazine or relaxing with the newspaper. Silence means still and without distractions.

Walking

If sitting still will never be your thing, you could try walking as your silent activity. You can take a brisk walk outside, but it may be even more effective to pace a small area where you can pay close attention to what your body is doing. As you would if you were practicing tai chi-chuan, which is a discipline of motion, notice your weight and how it moves. Notice how you plant your feet and how your muscles move. Stay focused on the movement of your body as a way to re-move the chatter from your mind.

Being in Nature

If the indoors is stifling, find a spot outside where you can sit or pace. When possible, remove shoes so you can feel the earth.

Candles

Lighting candles often sets the appropriate mood for silence and in-timacy. (The greatest love scenes would not be complete without candles. Why not set the scene for yourself?) Observe the flame to help yourself focus your mind. Imagine the radiance of the candle-light reflecting the same radiance you have inside. Internal radiance is the result of a successful session of silence.

Breathing

You may choose to focus on your breathing as a way to the silence. Follow your breath as it fills your lungs and as it is released through your nose or mouth. Observe it until your time is up or you have for-gotten to do so because you are in a Zen-like state. Try taking ten deep breaths to start this working for you. Inhale slowly, and exhale even more slowly. Silently count to four on the inhale, and eight on the exhale. Increase the number as you get better at it. Even if all you do is take these ten breaths before starting or ending your day, it will make a difference in your life.

Focus Through Touch

Stroking your cat or dog or feeling the smooth edge of a silk cord or satin blanket or smooth stone or other item of your choice may also help give your silence a focus. Use the stroking as a way to relax, let go, and stay in the silence.

GETTING TO THE
SILENCE: STARTERS

Here are some things that might help you make the sometimes difficult transition from your busy world to your silent world.

- Write down your distractions. Make your to-do list. Write down what you're worried about forgetting. Empty your mind onto a piece of paper. Then begin to find the silence.
- Spiritual reading. Keep a collection of poems, inspirational quotes, stories, or self-help literature close to the place where you have chosen to practice silence. Use a short reading to start shifting speeds in your mind.
- Gratitude. Mentally listing what you are grateful for will help shift you into a silence-ready mode.
- Prayer. If you have a religious prayer or even just one of your own making, this is a great way to begin being silent. Be careful not to spend the whole silent time praying, however, because the mental recitation does not allow for silence.

WISDOM IN ACTION

It's time to be silent. Aim for fifteen minutes of silence a day. Start with a shorter period if you need to, but do it! If you start small, gradually build up to fifteen minutes. Eventually, one day you'll be able to do twenty or thirty minutes a day or more.

Get started now. It's the next link to your best life! The trick is to expect nothing. Just do it.

Mastering silence is the first leg of a three-legged stool holding up your ability to master focus. Now let's look at the second leg: mastering your intentions.

YOUR INTENTIONS WILL
MAKE THEMSELVES KNOWN

Your intentions are the aim that guides your actions. When you intend to hit a target, you take the appropriate action toward it. Therefore, becoming a master of your intentions multiplies your chances
of creating what you want for yourself. We began looking at this issue
with Wisdom Access Questions and defining beliefs (see chapters 1
and 2). The next level covered here is to realize that it is possible to
want or take action on something, but have underlying intentions
that can undermine the whole process or can make the action you
meant to take less than effective. If you can monitor your motivation
and make sure it is in sync with the action you want to take, you
make the result easier to accomplish.

For this exploration, I use the words "motivation" and "intention"
interchangeably. When you have a hidden motivation or intent it can
mean one of two things: either you don't even know that your motivation is betraying what you are attempting to create, or a hidden
motivation could be something you *are* aware of, but are trying to
conceal from others.

The first kind of hidden motivation where you betray yourself
could be represented as follows: let's say you want to improve your
relationship with your spouse. You start taking action by being kinder
and making nurturing gestures such as cooking extraspecial meals or
showing up with gifts. Surprisingly, you can't understand why you
still want to lash out at your spouse. Soon you realize that although
you think you are taking action to improve the relationship and that
is what you would like, deep down you are still angry about past hurts
and intend to keep punishing your mate for them. You didn't even realize there was another motivation at work.

In the second kind of hidden intention, you can have an intention or motive that you think is not obvious to anyone but you. The
truth is even your hidden intentions can become obvious to others.
For example, if you dislike someone, despite your best efforts to
think otherwise, you may still find yourself wishing them ill. That is a

hidden intention. Although you behave to the contrary, your underlying motivation is to not like them. You will probably still continue to behave as if this is not true, but eventually, you will do or say something that would reveal your hidden feelings.

The key to mastering your intentions involves facing your negative intentions, those that don't serve what you are trying to create. It doesn't matter how hard you work to overcome a negative intention with positive action; if the hidden negative intention is there, it will work against you. On the other hand, combining positive intention and positive action yields results. Everything must align with the positive intention in order for it to come to fruition; every thought, word and action must be congruent. Focusing your intentions so they are positive and paying attention to your subsequent actions becomes critical to unearthing your best life.

Hidden negative intentions are tricky, though, so being aware of them is not that easy. They may crop up anyplace. If you become disappointed in how something is turning out, you may start unwittingly creating even more opportunities to move far away from the good thing you were trying to create. Do you beat yourself up? Do you start saying that nothing ever works out for you? Do you start believing you can't or won't ever see this thing come to fruition? All of these beliefs and messages become your new intent. In essence, you start to backtrack. And then you are contributing to making it impossible for your worthy intentions to come to be.

Neale Donald Walsch writes in *Conversations with God* (*Book One*), "Your life proceeds out of your intentions for it." Similarly, as you fall back into believing these negative thoughts, you plant the seeds for them to have power over you in measurable ways. You will be more likely to cling to these negative intentions than to try to turn them around in the name of something you cannot yet feel, see, or touch.

THE INTENTIONS QUIZ

Here's a quiz that will help you decipher the quality of your intentions and have clarity around hard-to-make decisions. Each question will uncover (or at least make you think about) whether you're harboring any potentially damaging intentions you might not even be aware of.

1. Does this idea/action benefit everyone around me as well as myself?
2. Will this idea/action serve as a tool for growth instead of a weapon against me or someone else?
3. Does withholding this information or knowledge or action represent a selfless instead of a selfish act?
4. Does this idea/action grow from wisdom instead of fear or doubt?
5. Does this idea/action stem from an internal desire instead of something I feel is expected of me or put upon me by others?

Count up how many yes answers you have. The more yeses, the purer your intention. Pure intentions are positive and born in your wisdom. They are more aligned with who you might ultimately want to be and also aligned with the ease with which you'll arrive where you are meant to be.

Some of the questions in the quiz above may sound lofty. I'm sure many of you can point to people who have cheated or manipulated their way to what they want, and you are pretty sure they got there without checking their true intentions. When I think about people like that I get angry and wonder whether I should just learn to be as slippery as they are. After all, they seem to get good results. But then I return to what I know—this is not who I am, therefore taking their path will only backfire. Your best bet is to keep this quiz close at hand, because it will help you focus your intentions so you can achieve them in a way you can be proud of. Part of your accomplishments should always be a sense of pride that they are deserved and that they came to you honestly.

You can still get what you want regardless of what your intention is, but the point is to carve out wisdom so you can experience accomplishment less painfully. Anything worth doing will challenge you and stretch you, but it doesn't need to affect your peace of mind to be worth it. By contrast, when we achieve out of negative intention, we get what we want only at a high emotional cost.

As I watch the change that is going on with people and the choices they are making about their lives and careers, I am seeing a shift. More and more people are judging their successes not by what they are earning or accumulating, but by what they had to give up to have it. That is what I mean by succeeding at the cost of your own peace. So many people are no longer willing to have their success outweighed by what they sacrificed to have it. They want more time with their families, more time for themselves and time in general to enjoy their lives. That is why work/life balance is a hot topic now as well as the simplicity movement and folks cashing in their 401(k)s early to go and live a less stressful existence. Of course, not all of us have that luxury, but the impetus to do so is gaining a quiet, yet forceful momentum.

Although most of my clients come to coaching for symptomatic reasons (for instance, wanting more money, a better job, or more time for their families), they almost all discover that if they truly listen to their quiet voice inside, the source of their dissatisfaction is a lack of meaning, satisfaction, and peace of mind. When they find the pure intention—what they truly want for themselves—their motivation is clear, so it is not difficult for them to follow through. The emotional cost of succeeding is lowered by finding your way to your positive intentions.

CHANGING THE INTENTION CAN LOWER THE COST OF SUCCESS

Michael was a family man, holding down a job, making time for his family, and doing good in his community. I suggested he take "The Intentions Quiz" at a time when he and his family were considering moving into a bigger, fancier home. When he checked his intentions against his desire for the showy home, he saw that he was being motivated by an old desire, one that had become his intention: to impress his parents, colleagues, and friends. He realized he always felt he had to project the image of the perfect husband, father, and provider. Suddenly, it was clear that buying the house was not an expression of himself or his family, but of a tangible reward that would then garner the expected praise.

When Michael realized that he was being motivated by values and expectations that were actually false for him, the anxiety he had had about not purchasing the house vanished. Instead, he was able to focus on making the home that his family already lived in meet all their needs in an even more satisfying way.

Taking a moment to consider his motives kept Michael from a purchase that could have been a big mistake. Buying a big house because it would make him look good, or because he felt it was expected of him, was not the foundation he wanted. He could have earned more money and afforded a big new home, but it would have been bought with false intentions. If he had gone through with it he might have missed the joy this purchase was supposed to create.

PROTECTING AN ILLUSION

Molly and Joe's housing problem was the opposite of Michael's. They had three kids, with a fourth on the way, and they were struggling to make ends meet. As we worked together on their budget, it was clear that their big, lovely home was a tremendous financial burden at the same time that it was the envy of family and friends. It was undeniable that moving to a smaller home would ease their fiscal pressures. Molly and Joe would have a nest egg from the sale of the old house and a smaller mortgage, lower utility bill, and so on would create a savings of $2,000 a month.

Although a move to a smaller house would create ease and financial safety in their lives, Molly and Joe were daunted by the prospect of having to tell the neighbors and their family and friends. Nonetheless, they saw that their intent—to create a higher quality of life—would be accomplished by this move, which would provide financial security. Staying in the big house would only be an illusion of a higher quality of life because in reality, the high expense of running the house curtailed their freedom. With their intentions clearly in sight, making the final decision to move was an easy choice.

I hope you are inspired to look at your intentions, for there is one more important reward you can reap by doing so. When you are a master at focusing your intentions in a positive way, they can become powerful enough to create results with *less* action—or sometimes even no action at all. When you have a powerful, positive intention rooted in wisdom and not ego, you can create an even greater magnet effect than what we discussed in the last chapter. For example, have you ever intended to get in touch with an old friend to connect and see how he or she is doing, only to bump into the friend or a third party who could get you in touch with the friend? Have you ever had a wish that you never really took any action toward nonetheless come true? That's the power of a big intention. It can't be something you are really attached to or may suffer over. However, it can be something big and perhaps improbable, but if you intend it deeply, it can come to be. For example, I never took any steps toward conceptualizing my search for a publisher for my first book. I had put it on my list of intentions in 1996 and by the end of the year, I was in negotiations for a book deal. Now, if I knew the magic formula for how to make this sort of thing happen over and over, I'd sell you the tonic—but for now just focus on clean, clear intentions and adjust your being to honor them. That is how great luck finds you.

STAY IN YOUR OWN LIFE

Our third and last leg of mastering focus comes in the form of focusing on your own life to find the answers to your blueprint. So many times we stay in limbo longer than needed because we compare ourselves to others or stray from our path because of what we see someone else doing. Worry, anxiety, comparison, or strain can result. Just pulling back from all the "noise" of our daily lives can provide clarity. By focusing on your own life, you can hear your wisdom. It may sound simple, but you can unearth the next step for you, regardless of what is going on around you.

Conventional wisdom says that when we want to accomplish something, we seek the advice of mentors or we follow the patterns of models who have achieved a similar goal already; it also suggests we become keen observers of how to accomplish what we want for ourselves. But sometimes, we can accidentally overload ourselves with so much information that we have a hard time processing what is applicable and true to our own situation.

So many people are driven to distraction by looking over the fence to see what their neighbors are doing. Accepting the pace of *your* life and taking care of it responsibly, as we discussed in chapter 5, will really make a difference in the long term, enabling you to get back to yourself and what you truly desire. This is what staying in your own life means.

Part of the Being and harnessing the resources of spirit includes this discipline of measuring yourself only in terms of your own life. When you spread your attention outward, gathering impressions of how life should be, you rob yourself of the wisdom your own life provides. Learn from others, but keep your own center as you layer that learning into your life. Try not to make the mistake of abandoning your own ship.

CLARITY IS IN YOUR OWN BACKYARD

Daria was a very successful public relations executive. She was very unhappy but felt she was doing the right thing: successful people worked hard and sacrificed a lot. This was especially true for those who did not have children, like Daria herself. It was only through working with her coach, Corrine Luessing (one of my InterCoach coaching partners), that she focused on her life and not on what everyone else was doing. Once she did this, it was clear that it made sense for her to leave her big firm and start her own business. Her new enterprise has thrived for two years without her even having to advertise or market herself.

Daria had also been under a big cloud of confusion when it came to the topic of having children. As she looked around and saw babies everywhere, she began to feel pressured and believed it was expected of her to have kids. She later admitted she stayed at her high-powered firm so long in part because it was acceptable there not to have kids. She felt she had created the image of a career woman who was riding too high on the career track to stop to have children. Nonetheless, once she focused on what *she* wanted, it was clear that kids were not in the picture. She no longer needed to hide behind her high-power job. She could face and accept her own truth. Daria and her husband agreed that a dog filled their nurturing needs and that it was okay not to have kids.

WISDOM IN ACTION

This is a good time to go back to Wisdom Access Questions (WAQs). Whenever you feel pulled to compare yourself to someone else or meet a benchmark because of what other people have accomplished, ask yourself the most powerful WAQ there is: "What do *I* want?"

Make this your mantra for several hours, or even a few days.

Don't force an answer—patiently wait for it to come to you (it will). The answer may not be in the form of a lightning bolt hitting you over the head; it may come as an inkling or a feeling, or it could become clear through a conversation with someone else.

It will also be particularly helpful to ask yourself what you want right before entering a period of silence.

WISDOM WRITING

Take out your wisdom journal or open your computer files, and use this time to examine your intentions. Look at the two or three goals or aspirations that are the most intense for you, based on all that we have covered so far. Give yourself "The Intentions Quiz" (p. 153) in writing for each one. Write out the questions and answer them for each burning goal. When you've uncovered your true intentions, determine whether your plan of action needs to be changed. If you discovered that the desire was not aligned with a healthy intention, change the desire to match an intention that is more positive. Take action.

WRAPPING IT UP WITH THE COACH

Now, we've begun the Being. This is where you begin to find the true satisfaction and peace that comes with living up to your best life. This is where we move from excavating your life blueprint to living it in harmony. To begin, you'll need to become a master at focusing.

You can do this by keeping the following in mind:

- Practice silence.
- Always check your true motives (your intentions).
- Change the action if you discover a negative motive.
- Stay in your own life.

ASK FOR DIRECTIONS
BEFORE YOU ARE LOST

You're driving to a destination you haven't been to in a while, but you're sure you remember the way. After all, you have a good sense of direction, and you're a great driver. You're almost there. You thought you knew your way around, but this time the roads just don't seem to be in the same place they were in last time. After driving up and down the same portion of road three times, finally you decide to ask for directions.

The same thing can happen in life. You thought you knew what to do at any given time, but after driving yourself crazy trying to make something work, you gave up and started asking for help to make it work.

In either case, what if you had asked for guidance before you set out of the gate? Well, for one thing, you'd probably be at your destination or someplace even better. Chances are that you'd have saved yourself time, trouble, and a great deal of energy and anxiety as well. Nobody likes being lost. By asking for help before you were lost, you could have spared yourself that unpleasant experience.

DIRECTIONS FROM INTUITION

Practicing silence and mastering focus opens you up to take advantage of a tremendous resource you may often overlook—your own intuition. The messages from your intuition are the directions you may not have thought to seek out.

In her *Practical Intuition*, Laura Day defines intuition as knowing without knowing why you know. It goes beyond what is explainable and asks you to bring all your senses to their highest potential. After the work you did in Part Two, "The Doing," you are more sensitive to physical clues and more aware of your own reactions to things and the sources of those reactions. Now you are ready to make it all come together.

Not using our intuition is a symptom of the fact that we use only a small portion of our brain. Yet, the source of intuition is not limited to your brain; it can come from other places, as we will discover. We will also explore how to use this tremendous resource to ease your way to your life blueprint. There is always the conventional way to assess what is possible, using the five senses: sight, sound, touch, feel, and smell. But expanding the scope of your intuition and the capacity to receive guidance in your life from a wiser, intangible part of yourself holds the promise of saving you unnecessary steps. It can keep you on track to your best life and even be more effective than logical, linear action when it comes to achieving a goal.

Expanding your intuition will take practice. You have to start building trust in your ability to use all the guidance available to you. It isn't easy to trust knowing without knowing why you know, but once you're successful a few times, I'm sure you won't go back to the old ways that left you lost before you asked for help.

WHERE DOES INTUITION COME FROM?

Sonia Choquette, in her book *The Psychic Pathway*, explains that there are three places that your intuitive inklings come from: the subconscious mind, group consciousness, and the superconscious or spiritual connections. I am going to give you good reasons to consider using these three sources of intuition as viable options for making choices in your life, if you have yet to include your intuitive side in your life. (If you already do, we'll be taking your use of intuition to the next level.)

What are the characteristics of each of the three sources of intuition?

Intuition from the Subconscious

Your subconscious mind holds all the information you've learned, acquired, and experienced. When your brain is searching for an answer or guidance on something, it may look to the subconscious, the corners too obscure for your conscious self to recognize. As we focus on using our intuition, what becomes interesting is that the subconscious will take old information and form a new relationship to it. We may then use it to guide us.

Bringing up information from the subconscious is like rediscovering a forgotten possession in your basement. It becomes new again and serves you in ways it did not before. For example, suddenly remembering a childhood poem that you haven't thought of in thirty years might give you the perfect sentiment to share with an ailing friend.

Intuition from Collective Consciousness

Have you ever been standing in traffic, felt drawn to look at the person in the next car, and caught that person staring back at you? We are connected in our thoughts to other people, whether we choose to believe it or not. You turn your head to look into the next car because you somehow feel that other person's gaze or sense his presence. You knew to turn *without knowing why you knew.*

When we ask for directions, sometimes we are tapping into a collective consciousness of information that comes to us in the form of an intuitive hit or inkling. Collective consciousness is the same principle that makes it possible to sometimes heal people through a prayer chain, or to think you came up with a unique, secret idea only to find your friend halfway around the world from you had the very same thought. The collective consciousness is a pool of information we can all tap into for guidance.

Intuition from the Superconscious or the Spiritual

Whether you believe in a higher source or not, we have all admitted at one time or another that some events, coincidences, and synchronicities cannot be explained by logic alone. So, if it isn't logical or rational, let's agree it came from the superconscious, the part of us in touch with what can only be reached beyond our own souls.

An intuitive inkling from the superconscious, especially when you are not used to asking it for directions, will probably feel somewhat alien to you. Your intuition will probably tell you to do or say something or go somewhere that may seem out of character for you. The direction may not appear logical, but following it can have a payoff. The prize for doing so will usually be an insight, result, or idea that makes complete sense once you've heeded your intuition's direction.

I remember going on an out-of-character camping trip to Alaska (hotels and room service were my preference). While I was there, my intuition told me to abandon the planned route I had prepared for my daily hike. As uncomfortable as I was in not charting a course, I let my feet follow my intuition. I was not afraid, but I remember sensing a suspended reality as I let myself be guided by something intangible. Nonetheless, when I came across a field of mystical-looking quartz crystal and, later, a herd of sheep, mothers and babies that let me sit among them in silence, I experienced an overwhelming feeling of connection with nature and life.

These discoveries still rate as among the most magical moments in my life. I also walked away with a big lesson about the value of being flexible when it comes to any plan. I saw how often something better than what *you* can plan or build can be waiting for you if you're open to it.

Intuition is as innate as the wisdom that I hope by now I have confirmed you possess. Some people may think intuition and wisdom are virtually interchangeable. I don't; so let's take a minute to make the distinctions between them clear. Intuition is the data, the intuitive realization of a possiblity. Wisdom is what you do with it. Acting on your intuition is following your own wisdom. Learning from the times your interpretation of your intuition was not quite accurate is also wisdom. If wisdom is the memory of the soul, then intuition is the funnel of information that empties into you for your wisdom to process. All the impressions and information comes to you through your intuition and wisdom helps you act on it.

Our journey to unearthing the blueprint to your best life has been about shedding the obstacles that keep your own wisdom at bay. One of those obstacles has been remaining unaware of your intuition. By examining how to tap into your intuition and understanding how to weave it into your life, you'll soon be able to rely on your intuition instead of ignoring it.

HOW TO RECEIVE AND ACCEPT INTUITIVE GUIDANCE

How do you lead a life that includes intuition and direction from less than concrete, logical sources? There are four steps.

Be Open to Intuition

Your work practicing silence and taking care of your life responsibly sets you up to hear what has always been lying right beneath the surface of logic and fact. When problems are at a minimum and your mind is quieter, there is room for your intuition to come through. However, you must be a believer to have it find you. Suspend judgment and trust the freefall this brings.

Expect Intuition

Give up the notion that everything is in your control when it comes to creating your best life. Expect to co-create that life with your world by listening to its guidance. This takes the burden off you and gives life a flow that you will begin to trust.

Ask for Guidance from Your Intuition

Later in this chapter, I'll show you how to ask for guidance and intuitive messages in writing, but you can also do it verbally whenever you want. Ask the wiser part of you what you need to know about a specific concern or what you need to do about a specific situation. Be sensitive when waiting for an answer. It may come as something you hear, feel, or see; it may even be something you interpret from a dream or that someone else tells you.

I use this with something as simple as finding my keys. I ask myself, "Where are my keys?," take a deep breath, and wait for what occurs to me. I usually find my keys when I follow that next thought.

Act on Your Intuition

Intuitive inklings are wasted when they are not acted upon. Although they may direct you to stretch beyond your comfort zone, and even if you do not get the result you expect, acting on an inkling will help you learn about yourself. Remember, your intuition is designed for your own good.

WISDOM IN ACTION

What Occurs to You?

The best way to start you off on using your intuition or to take it to the next level is to raise your awareness to the point where you start noticing every thought that occurs to you. You can begin by taking a day or you can work on this for a week. Every time you have a thought or inclination to call someone, do something, wear something, or try something, I want you to do it. It is paramount to remember that these inklings of intuition will seem free of emotion and feel very neutral. If what occurs to you is destructive in any way—eating that extra dessert, telling someone what you *really* think of them, cheating your way around a problem—then it is *not* your intuition trying to speak to you. Those are negative thoughts that don't count for this exercise.

To come to trust your intuition, track what occurs to you, act on the positive inklings (even if they don't make sense), and watch which ones result in helpful guidance. Even an inkling to wear a favorite ring might become significant when it becomes a great conversation-starter with someone you've been eager to meet and you finally get the chance on this particular day.

The difference between this process and the Blank Day exercise in chapter 4 is that this one goes further. Now you are going beyond what you want, to a point where you are allowing intuitive guidance to lead you to something out of your conscious awareness that might be best for you.

THE ENEMY OF INTUITIVE GUIDANCE

We established earlier that fear is the greatest obstacle to any wisdom trying to reach us. The same holds true with intuition. In order to act on intuition, you'll need to distinguish between the intuition itself and when fear is getting in the way.

Fear can often talk to you in harsh ways. Intuition would never do that. Even if you don't listen to intuition at first, it will always linger in the gentlest of ways. Maybe a nagging feeling would be intuitive guidance at its worst, but it would not get worse than that. Intuition will always be gentle, fear will not.

For example, being afraid to fly in an airplane might give you the jitters, make you anxious and upset for days before a trip, or even evoke dreams of nightmarish terror associated with planes and flying. But if your intuition were trying to send you a warning and directing you to not go on a plane, it would nudge you to change the reservation or you'd get the feeling that you'd better go on this trip another time. Intuition will not terrorize you, but it will direct you.

INTUITIVE GUIDANCE FOR A
RELUCTANT PARTICIPANT

Michelle had done everything "right"—attended good college, found a good job as a scientist, been singled out for praise at the corporation where she worked—and yet harbored a secret dissatisfaction with her life. She longed for a more extroverted career, specifically as a trainer, teaching adults in corporations. However, Michelle's scientifically trained mind, used to needing proof and concrete evidence, could not allow her to make the leap to follow her desire.

When she was about to be promoted again, Michelle hired me as a coach under the auspices of wanting to start her new job off on the right foot. It didn't take long to uncover her dream of changing careers, but it took a lot of prodding before she would take action. It wasn't until an "inexplicable" depression started to set in that Michelle was willing to explore the possibility of moving on to what was calling her.

Michelle finally accepted my suggestion that she inquire about the requirements to become an in-house trainer. The training director echoed all her rational doubts: "You have no background in training. You have to at least take some courses. You need experience." Michelle retreated, feeling a strange mix of rejection and satisfaction, the latter from knowing she had been justified in surpressing this desire.

The very same week, Michelle "coincidentally" met a man at her gym named Gary. A trainer for a large consulting firm, he also volunteered at a program that taught life skills to inner-city kids. Intrigued, she expressed interest in helping with the program, but when Gary called to follow up, she backed away from making a commitment.

Within two weeks Michelle found herself lost in an unfamiliar part of the city and pulled into a crowded school parking lot to find someone to ask directions. Lo and behold, who did she see but Gary. On his way to lead one of his classes for the kids, he invited her in to take a peek.

Intrigued by seeing the program in action, this time Michelle actually volunteered to help with administration. As a result, she got a chance to observe the course several times. One Saturday, Gary called Michelle from his car; he was stuck in a huge traffic jam, and he was not going to make it to the kids' course on time, if at all. He begged Michelle to take his place. Despite her initial resistance, Michelle had no choice but to lead the class.

As it turned out, Michelle was a hit—the kids loved her. Gary invited Michelle to lead the class as often as she wanted to. He was very impressed with her warmth and her natural teaching abilities. Buoyed by his praise and inspired by watching how well Gary could work with adults and kids, Michelle once more felt encouraged to pursue her dream of becoming a trainer.

About six months later, Gary recommended Michelle to his boss. She interviewed for a position at Gary's company, and he promised to be available to mentor her. Michelle was offered the trainer's job, and quickly accepted. She was on her way.

Michelle's intuition about changing careers was more stubborn than she was. Once she admitted the truth about what she wanted, she was unleashing wisdom. Despite the fact that she was resistant to taking action, the path to her fulfillment found her. The coincidences involved—meeting Gary at the gym, running into him in the inner city—were life's way of guiding her until she could no longer deny her life blueprint.

THE LITERAL VERSUS THE SYMBOLIC

Learning to distinguish intuition from fear will increase your intuitive hits. You'll also become better and better at interpreting some of the less literal messages your intuitive guidance is trying to deliver. Very few people will receive the kind of guidance that involves hearing very real, distinct voices or seeing images in their mind telling them what to do. People with that level of sensitivity move into psychic spheres of clairaudience or clairvoyance. For most of us, it will usually come in the form of a thought, a feeling, or a dream. It may even be something more obviously attention-grabbing, such as five people telling you to read the same book, until you finally get the message and succumb to the purchase. However, not all guidance will be literal. Some you may have to interpret. This will mean recognizing some of the less obvious signs that your intuition is trying to reach you. These signs will often be symbolic.

For example, my best friend, Carolynn, has a strong symbolic attachment to sunflowers. They remind her of her deceased father, because they were his favorite flower. Not only is she reminded of him, but depending on what is going on in her life at the time, the flower can represent that her dad is sending guidance. It seems a strong coincidence that whenever she's confused about something, she may notice a sunflower in a shop window, on a postcard on someone's desk, or on the sweater of a child in a passing car. It doesn't matter what form it comes in, but when she sees a sunflower, it symbolically reminds her of her dad. It also makes her consider what he would say about her dilemma. This is usually enough to jog her out of confusion and into clarity. The symbol reminds her to tune in to herself and the answer.

Similarly, for me, the simple raising of the hairs on my arm tells me symbolically that I have heard or spoken a deep truth. When that happens, I know not to ignore what was just said, but to pay special attention to it, and to proceed from that realization to the proper course of action.

WISDOM IN ACTION

Take notice of any symbols you have come to recognize in your life as meaningful. If you do not have any, keep this in the forefront of your attention for a couple of days, trying to notice things that seem significant to you in terms of guidance. They will usually represent positive impressions instead of negative ones.

I hope you realize I am not talking about superstition. No black cats or rabbit's feet. I want to guide you to find symbolic benchmarks that will help heighten your own trust in your intuition. The symbols are highly personal and only you can recognize them. They are like pats on the back from your intuition, which say, Yup, you're on the right track. Look for them and start using them whatever they may be, whatever area of your life they may come from.

INTUITION IS NOT AN EXACT SCIENCE

There is such a thing as going too far with interpreting your intuition and the meaning of everything that happens to you. Don't become a slave to intuition. That's the same as believing your doctor, your tarot card reader, or your child's teacher is always right.

Intuition is not an exact science, and your intuitive inklings are open to interpretation. However, your interpretation won't always be right (although you'll get better at it over time) and not everything has to have huge significance. Sometimes things just are the way they are because they are.

If trying to come up with an interpretation of an event or an inkling or a dream causes you to suffer or get down on yourself, stop! Don't force it. Guidance is supposed to be gentle (if you need that lesson reinforced, go back to our discussion of entering "the zone" on page 81). If an answer or an interpretation is not forthcoming, give it time—it might show up later, when you least expect it, or not at all.

Just use what you have learned in this chapter to enhance your life, not to make it more complicated.

WISDOM WRITING

This writing assignment will be different from anything we've done so far, but that is because it comes in the advanced part of the journey toward your best life.

Until now you've explored things in writing, maybe even written a letter to yourself. Now we are going to raise the stakes and improve your intuitive sense by writing to a wiser part of you. You can call it your higher self, the wise mind, or—as some of my workshop participants have—your wisewoman or wiseman.

Using WAQs again, address an issue you would like guidance on by asking your wiser mind questions. Do this exercise with only one issue at a time. It can be about anything that is frustrating you or about the specific meaning of an event in your life. If you need help, consult the list of questions in Appendix 2.

Write to your wise mind until you have asked all your questions and expressed all your frustration about the issue: "What do I need to know about dealing with X?" you may ask. Or, "What am I overlooking to make this goal happen?" Or, "What good is supposed to come out of the anger I feel about X?" Continue asking until you feel ready to hear an answer. Then take a moment to breathe deeply, and clear those questions of any emotions with another deep breath, and when you feel you are in a neutral place emotionally, pick up your pen again.

Now let your wise mind write back. You may think that you are making up the answers you want to hear or that this exercise is silly or contrived, but do it anyway. Just write what occurs to you. Write until you feel you have nothing else to say.

When you read what you've written, there should be nuggets of wisdom for you to act on or contemplate. If not, do not throw them away. Often time will be your greatest measure as to the accuracy of your wise mind's predictions and answers. I am constantly amazed at how silly I feel doing this writing, only to read what I have written months later, in awe at how the guidance I received from my very own self was true, productive, and sometimes miraculous.

Notice the voice that speaks back to you in the writing. I would bet it's kinder and more caring than the inner critic you may have. Many workshop participants have talked about the lack of a punishing, negative voice, and how they feel they've found a friend in themselves through this writing.

Use this exercise as often as you like to tap into the wiser part of you. For many, it becomes a daily ritual.

WRAPPING IT UP WITH THE COACH

By using intuition to ask for directions and guidance before you need help, you can tap into all the resources available to you as you become more attuned to your blueprint and its payoff of a happy, fulfilled life.

- Notice what occurs to you.
- Be open to intuition.
- Ask for guidance from it.
- Act on your intuition.
- Recognize symbols that intuitive clues are trying to reach you.
- Write to your wise mind regularly.

GIVE UP NEEDING
TO KNOW

W HAT DO YOU NEED TO KNOW TO HAVE THE LIFE THAT YOU want? Do you need to know how to make a living? Do you need to know how to be a loving parent? Do you need to know how to make a million dollars? What is it that you feel you must know in or-der to get what you want?

Let me answer for you:

You do not need to know *anything* specifically. You just need to know that you have the inner authority to not let yourself down.

So many people feel they cannot have what they want until they get another degree, become fully accomplished in something, or are absolutely certain of what they want out of their life. However, these are not prerequisites for success, satisfaction, or happiness. In fact, knowledge can be limiting—it can hinder possibility.

If you know women only make seventy-five cents on the dollar that men earn, then you may find yourself defined and limited by that fact. You may not ask for more, even though you feel you deserve it, or may limit yourself in some other way. Yes, sometimes ignorance can be bliss. If I had known that my first book, *Take Yourself to the Top,* was in a book genre that normally is not expected to exceed sales of ten to fifteen thousand copies, I would have never even dreamed of selling a million copies. I have not reached that number—yet!—

but book sales sure went way above what was expected, because of my dedication to making the book sell, my public appearances, my grass-roots efforts, *and* because I did not *know* any better. Because I didn't know any better, I did everything I could to make that book sell, and it did.

We grasp at knowledge because we have been trained to believe that knowledge is power and with that power we hope to find security. This is another major stumbling block to the wisdom that wants to come through to guide your life. The greatest security comes in trusting yourself enough to not be fazed by the unknown. We will look at that true security in this final section of our work on the Being.

Gail Sheehy, the author of *Passages,* said it best: "Creativity can be described as letting go of certainty." Not knowing gives us the freedom to create. If I were to guess at the thing that keeps people the most dissatisfied with their lives, it would be the loss of their creativity. Whether it's their marriage, their job, or life in general, when things become mundane—when we have fallen into a routine and are merely doing what we know—we lose that spark that gives our lives wings.

My first coach, Jay Perry, said, " 'I don't know' is a great opportunity for creativity." So finding the wisdom in uncertainty gives us the experience of ourselves that we long for. We are creative beings. When we experience the power of creating something where there was nothing before, we feel a tremendous sense of power. That power—not the power of knowledge, but the power of creating our own lives from the fiber of our own being—is our creative life force.

When we cling to the notion that knowledge is the only way we can have that power, we lessen what we are capable of. Knowing or knowledge can also lead to prejudice and snobbery, both of which paralyze parts of us. You may miss out on a fulfilling friendship or experience because you have prejudged the outcome by thinking you know the reputation of the person you're about to meet or the reputation of the company you might have been thinking of joining. Thinking you know can make you jaded.

Think of going to see a revival of a famous Broadway play. If it's a classic you've read or seen before, why go? Perhaps you would go to discover nuances you might have missed, to pick up something unexpected, or to be open to a new interpretation by the director or the actors. Not knowing and just going for the ride is a huge part of reaching the satisfaction and fulfillment of your life blueprint.

I'm not advocating that you forget everything you've ever learned and become a blank slate. The knowledge that you've gained is an integral part of you, and certain skills you've been taught, such as how to balance a checkbook, are higly desirable things to hold on to. For the exploration in this chapter, however, the blueprint you need to excavate isn't always rooted in what you know, and a lack of knowledge shouldn't be used as an excuse for not taking action on what you desire. As you explore the concept of not needing to know, you will realize how much you rely on what you know instead of using who you are to make a difference. The payoff to relying more on who you are than on what you know includes deeper relationships, more innovative solutions to everyday problems, and an increased sense of self.

WISDOM IN ACTION

To start you on the way to being comfortable with not knowing, spend the next twenty-four hours free of having answers. In other words, refuse to be the expert on anything for a day. Refrain from answering any query you're asked, be it by your kids, spouse, coworkers, or even your own self. When appropriate, respond with: "I'll have to get back to you on that." Or ask the person a question that would help him come up with the answer himself (try using Wisdom Access Questions).

Or, instead of jumping in with an answer, ask him what he thinks the answer is. You will be amazed at how many times the other person can answer his own question if given the chance.

Regardless of how you deflect the question, the point is for you to experience the inquiry that ensues when you allow yourself to "not know." Notice how you behave differently. Notice how you feel. Notice how your creativity and conversation with others change. Does it make you feel more secure or insecure to not know? Record your impressions in your wisdom journal.

HOW "NOT KNOWING" LEADS TO OPPORTUNITY

Tony had a very nice position at American Express and loved the people he worked with. He made a great salary, he was well liked, and he had been promoted a series of times, but he felt something was missing and that his creativity had been shut down by the routine and lack of challenge. Working with InterCoach coach Jeanne McLennan, Tony found that helping others and contributing to the development of people was the part of his work he enjoyed the most. However, he did this for only part of his day, and that wasn't enough for him to feel fully alive at his job.

Jeanne introduced Tony to one of my favorite organizations, Future Possibilities, a nonprofit group that matches inner-city kids with a coach, so that he might fulfill his need to help others. Tony did not know how to coach or how to deal with kids, but it appealed to him so he trained to be a volunteer coach. During his training, as he observed how everyone in the group was respectful and really believed in its mission, he felt compelled to get more involved.

Before he even knew what hit him, Tony had taken a sabbatical from American Express, on half pay. He wasn't sure how he would make ends meet, but he felt he could afford the risk. By the time the six months were up, he was in conversation with the executive director of Future Possibilities, who was preparing to change her role, about becoming its next leader. The position was unlike anything he had done before, nor did he know much about nonprofits, but Tony decided to leave his job to assume the executive director position. He says he now feels energized and has a sense of purpose.

Tony is not sure what the future holds, but he is on the board of several start-up businesses, is training to improve his coaching skills, and has a plan he thinks will work for him. The people around him have told him he seems happier, he and his girlfriend have gotten engaged, and his family and friends are rooting for him like they never have before. Not knowing what was coming was the perfect way for Tony to begin to discover how to live his best life.

LEAPS OF FAITH

The philosopher Immanuel Kant writes convincingly about the leap of faith necessary to believe, to do, or to be, but you don't need to become a great thinker to realize anything worth having, doing, or even being takes a leap of faith to get to.

Giving up the need to know also includes taking leaps of faith. You may not be sure of an outcome, but you can trust the decision to move forward if you know you'll somehow land on your feet. Having a difficult conversation with someone, starting a business from scratch, or changing careers in midlife are all courageous moves that require leaps of faith.

What is keeping you from taking a leap of faith? For most of us, it is that common enemy, fear.

Let's take a moment to put some structure around deciding whether to take a leap of faith or not. How do you know when it's okay to not know what the outcome will be, and still take a leap of faith?

PULL MAKES YOU WILLING, PUSH MAKES IT HARD

When it comes to leaps of faith, things that call to you, that propel you, or that somehow pull you toward them seem to work out better than things you are pushing to make happen. Wisdom will always pull you; it will never push you. You need to let yourself feel the subtle difference between pushing for a result and being pulled to accomplish one.

Many of my clients have questions about this concept. How do you want something and yet not push for it? Does that mean you don't go after it? Does that mean you pretend you don't want it? Does that mean let the other person or parties make the first move? The answer to these last three questions is a resounding no, and it doesn't mean you should settle or sit in your room and visualize it into existence, either.

The way to get something without pushing for it is to take appropriate action, but always watch yourself to make sure you're not trying too hard. If you find yourself scheming, plotting, or second-guessing yourself and everyone else, as well as attempting to manipulate a situation in your favor, you are pushing. The energy it takes to push for a result chokes the faith out of any leap, and makes it hard, although not impossible, to get results. It's simply that it takes great effort and often there's no sense of enjoyment in the doing. It becomes difficult because of fear. You are afraid that you won't ultimately lead your best life without this thing, so you try to manipulate your world to *make* it happen.

On the other hand, if you feel pulled by something or moved to passionately pursue something even against great odds and obstacles, keep going. As long as you are not hurting yourself or anyone else in the process, it is wisdom prodding you. When you are pulled by something, it will usually be something that has a greater purpose than your own material satisfaction. Even if it is not, it most likely allows for the kind of personal fulfillment that is in itself a great contribution to your world. Often, taking a stand for the better part of yourself—or for something that serves more than your purposes—allows for the magical results that defy explanation. The leap of faith is rewarded.

A leap of faith requires not knowing what the result will be. It is a dance. The perfect dance partner doesn't step on her counterpart's toes. If your partner is trying to control you instead of lead you, he will definitely make it an erratic dance. The perfect dance partner stands awaiting the cue and responding in an imperceptible second. That is the dance of pull. You need to be the ideal partner.

BEING PULLED TO FLY

My brother Paul is a great example of push/pull in life. At eighteen, he enrolled in our father's alma mater, Purdue University, and set off determined to do well. However, he slogged his way through the first year, barely getting by no matter how hard he tried. Our parents were pressuring him, and he pushed himself to do better. Still it was fruitless. I watched him close down, moving perfunctorily through the motions but numb even to his own self-criticism.

Interestingly enough, he was failing school because all he could do was find time for being in a biplane on a friend's nearby farm learning to fly. The pull of flying felt like freedom to my brother. Literally, he told me, he felt the freedom of flight; up in the air, he also lacked the heaviness of what he had been pushing himself to do in his life on the ground.

My brother flunked out of both Purdue and a community college. Only when he returned as an aviation engineering major did he excel at Purdue, graduating with honors. Paul recognized that he was pulled toward flying and he literally soared to success. He's now a commercial pilot and is still pulled to learn more about mastering his craft.

My brother's example shows what happens when we try to push ourselves to do something we don't really want to do, instead of giving up needing to know, free-falling, and letting ourselves be pulled by something we may discover is just right for us.

To see what happens when we are pushing for something we *do* want, something we want badly, let's look at my client Marta. She had spent a lot of money marketing her services as an interior designer, but she had yet to see a profit in the five years she'd been in business, much less enough money to draw a salary. We put several strategies into place that made a difference, yet the doors seemed to be slamming shut in her face.

My experience told me that the service she was offering and giving to those who hired her was not the problem, the strategies were not the problem, but that Marta herself was the problem. She was pushing too hard. She worked seven days a week, despite my requests that she take evenings and weekends off and go on vacation now and again. Her results were not commensurate with her effort. Although she couldn't even feel the difference between push and pull, I'm sure her prospective clients could feel it: we tend not to buy from pushy, desperate people; we buy from people who exude ease and confidence.

It has been a few years since we worked together, but Marta never did stop pushing. As a result, despite her toil and growing Rolodex of contacts, prosperity has eluded her.

To be honest about my stage career, I was pushing for success. Every actor has to hustle and be out there to attract opportunity, but there was no ease about what I was doing. I was consumed by it, plotting move after move. Instead of singing a song that I loved for an audition, I would try to second-guess what the producers wanted to hear. Sometimes that worked, but most of the time it left me exhausted and unemployed.

However, when I committed to building a coaching practice, I wasn't pushing. Instead, I was so happy to find something I loved that fit the way I wanted to live, I felt pulled. Opportunities to be featured in the media, and the endorsement of influential people seemed to find me. Other than being 100 percent committed and enthusiastic about what coaching could do for people, I did nothing to make these things happen. I'm not implying that I didn't work hard or that there weren't problems along the way, but I was careful not to push. If I felt tempted by the push trap, I'd remember the pain my last career had caused me, and I would stop. My eventual success was a combination of effort and trust. It was definitely a leap of faith, but I felt I was doing the right thing for me, my marriage, and the family my husband and I were intent on having. What really gave me the courage to keep leaping, even if there was doubt, was feeling that my success would contribute to the new profession that it was at that time.

Being pulled by something feels much different than pushing for it. Pull is less tiring than push. Pull is like entering a party that welcomes you. Push is showing up at the party unannounced, and then having to make your way through a crowd—your weight moves people but it's a major struggle to part the throng so you can pass. Similarly, pushing for a result will throw the balance out some-where—somewhere along the line, it will stop working. When you feel pulled, you don't need to push.

Are you ready for a leap of faith? Check the pull-versus-push factor. They may both be scary, but a pull will feel compelling where a push will cause you to feel driven. Make sure it's a pull before you leap. The odds of landing safely are better.

TIMING

Am I being lazy, or is it really not the right time? That is what I hear when things aren't going exactly as someone planned. There is really only so much we can control and when we know we have done our best to make something happen, then all we can do is wait. That is the hardest part. However, coming to know the difference be-tween waiting patiently for something to happen and being lazy is a big part of being comfortable with not knowing and developing trust in yourself.

My first coach told me, "Even when you are not doing your best, you are doing your best." I interpreted this to mean that although I know I have done better, if this is all I can do now, it is the best I can do for now. That may sound like a nice positive spin to get yourself off the hook, but there is no question that forgiving yourself for your momentary lapse in excellence is much more productive than con-stantly berating yourself.

The standard I recommend is taking an honest look at the effort you've made. If you have done everything you can think of (including getting outside, additional support) to attack a project or desired goal, than it is time to let it rest. Let the power of that effort have some time to mature. Maybe you'll find a better way later, or maybe it was meant to show you something else about yourself but never come to be.

If you are not in action, and if you are hiding from what you say you want, then you are sabotaging your efforts. You know deep down when fear is getting the best of you. Cut the goal down to a bite-size piece you can chew off now.

The other possible approach would be to reexamine your goal to ensure it is really something you truly want. If it doesn't feel that way, the goal may very well be something you felt you *should* do. Leaps of faith cannot come from "shoulds."

WISDOM STORY: MEET ALISON
BEING PULLED TO LEAP NOW!

When Alison attended one of my seminars, she was between jobs and figuring she needed to get a temp job. But Alison had a great sense of design and a dream to produce unusual greeting cards from photographs she had collected. She had neither business experience nor a lot of money, but she felt pulled to her idea and she felt the time to start was now.

Many of Alison's friends and family thought she was crazy for taking such a big chance, but she did not let naysayers stop her. She was scared and she was flirting with financial disaster, but she chose to go full steam ahead. In a few months, she had designed her entire line of cards, had them placed in shops, and was selling them online through her website. Today, her business is still in the start-up stage, but it is growing steadily.

Although logic would dictate that Alison could have reduced the risk by taking a temp job, and she herself will admit she had no guarantee of a positive outcome, she trusted herself and knew that even if she failed she'd find a way to rally again. That attitude and confidence is the way of wisdom and the fuel that accelerates the blueprint to your best life.

WISDOM IN ACTION

Here is a cliché you can really use: There is no time like the present.

Put down this book and take one action toward something you've always wanted to do. It doesn't have to be a major life-changing leap of faith; it can be something as simple as a new hairstyle, learning a new sport, hobby, or computer skill, or anything that has been long stuck on the back burner. Whatever it is, trust that there is some reason you are drawn to do it now and make a move toward doing it.

Once you do, take a moment to observe what you learned from what you did or tried to do, how it helped you grow, and what possibilities it opened for you. You wouldn't think that finally trying golf would radically alter your life, but there could be more to learn from it than the mechanics of the game. You may find that you could push yourself further physically than you thought, or that you are better at strategy than you believed. These insights are the wisdom to be gained from taking that particular leap. Trust that there is a reason you were drawn to it, regardless of how practical it may be.

For instance, I once participated in a ceremonial firewalk. On my first try walking the coals barefoot, I got burned. I was determined to try again because I didn't intend to do another ceremony like this again. The leader asked me to walk this time for "something bigger than yourself." I silently decided to walk for generations of happiness in my family. I sailed across the coals as if I were elevated three feet above them.

This was not something I need to do again, but as a leap of faith, it made me understand the power of using your life for something bigger than your own goals. In that way, the one-time experience of firewalking has shaped my life since.

Regardless of what you reach to try, record your impressions of your experience in your wisdom journal.

GIVING UP CONTROL

At some point during this work we are doing together, I hope that you started to feel a bit lost. As you evolve toward the life you are meant to live, you may start feeling a bit disoriented because you've begun to let go of controlling every aspect of what happens to you. That is how you know you are living in your human "beingness" versus your human "doingness."

The purpose of this book is to help you grow beyond the life you think you want to your best life. The wisdom that comes from giving up the need to know allows you to move more freely toward that best life. Not knowing speeds up the evolution of your life and yourself because there is no preconceived notion to struggle with. You look at responsibility differently. You build a strong foundation by getting your life to work, as you've done throughout the course of this book, so you are then able to let go, expecting the best and yet well prepared to endure the worst.

Preparing your life for success this way reminds me of how actors prepare for a play. For the intense period of rehearsals, they learn their lines, work out their movements on the stage with their fellow actors, live the text, and breathe the text. On opening night, however, they let go. Confident that they've done their homework, they forget all the details of the weeks of rehearsal. Now the performance belongs to the synchronicity of the moment. The actors have their technique and the experience of rehearsals as their foundation, but the best performance happens in the moment. So does your best life.

After doing the work in these three stages of unearthing your life's blueprint, you are poised for your best life. You've done the work, you've set the stage, and now you let the Being part of you take over. You've now stepped into the power you have to create your own life.

WISDOM WRITING

This is the last writing exercise of our present journey together. Simply write about your impressions about who you are now compared to who you were when you began this book.

Also take a moment to look at your first writing entry, about where you were in your life and what you were hoping to accomplish. Have you arrived? Is the aim completely different? What have you learned? How did you grow?

Chances are your goals have changed by now, or at least they've changed in their significance.

WRAPPING IT UP WITH THE COACH

When you give up needing to know, you have reached the ultimate level of trust in yourself. Here are some tips to keep in mind as you integrate this strategy into your life:

- Value creativity and possibility over knowledge.
- Practice not knowing by asking more questions.
- Measure the pull against the push and take a leap of faith.
- Measure laziness against patience and trust in the perfect timing.
- Do what you want to do and watch what you learn.

Finally, here's an anonymous quotation I found that sums up the point of this chapter: "Knowledge is proud that it has learned so much. Wisdom is humble that it knows no more."

CONCLUSION
THE RECKONING,
THE DOING, AND THE BEING:
LIVING YOUR BEST LIFE

H OW WILL YOU KNOW IF YOU ARE LIVING YOUR LIFE BLUE-
print? The simple answer is that you'll be happy and feel
tremendous gratitude for your life, even if you are still working
toward your dreams. If that doesn't give you enough information,
there are other ways to help determine whether you have reached
the point of living your best life. Ask yourself these questions:

- Are you future- and solution-oriented, instead of past- and
  problem-focused?
- Do you catch yourself falling into negative beliefs and know how
  to reverse them?
- Do you have more satisfying relationships because you keep
  conflict in perspective?
- Do you recognize the unacceptable and take immediate action
  to change it?
- Are you aware of how you make a difference in the world, re-
  gardless of your life's status or job description?
- Do you have more than enough time for the things that really
  matter to you?
- Are you attracting opportunities, seemingly without effort?
- Can you move through problems and crises with more ease?

- Are you taking more chances, ones that move your life forward in a positive way?
- Do you have deep respect for who you are, and design your life to suit yourself?

If the majority of your answers are yes, you are well on the way to living your life blueprint.

You've now entered a whole new dimension in living—living your best life. You've progressed through the Reckoning, the Doing, and the Being, and if you've read this book in the manner that I hope you have, it should deliver you to where you are meant to be. Only you can know if you've arrived there, although, if you set a preconceived notion of what this would be, you probably found you were wrong. To paraphrase the advertising tag of the movie *Beautiful*: Sometimes you have to give up the dream of your life to have the life of your dreams. Which means we often don't know where we are meant to be until we arrive there.

Your best life (where you are meant to be) is a life where you can take the good with the bad, experience a lot of love, and feel that you are fully expressed in the world without being anyone or anything other than your truest self. When you commit to following the strategies in this book, you will arrive at your best life by creating the circumstances by which great luck can find you. Letting this luck in requires being specific about what you want, what is ideal for you, and what must be let go from your present life to have those things. However, being open to luck also requires the detachment of being open to something greater and even better than what you can imagine.

The process that we have undergone together takes work and is an ongoing evolution. I recommend you come back to this book for a reference course in wisdom whenever you're feeling tested and challenged. It will be particularly helpful if you feel you've lost your center—as we often do when life throws us a completely new set of circumstances. These curveballs are also a part of the blueprint, but the more you practice this work, the easier and faster you will get back on track to your best life.

To maintain what you've accomplished here, keep these things in mind:

- Be responsible for your thoughts, words, and deeds.
- Decide *who* you want to be before deciding *what* you'll do.
- Cooperate with your world by taking action.
- Be grateful for what is (even if you do not like it).
- Behave as if the result has already arrived.

In *Trends 2000,* Gerald Celente predicted that "confronted by necessity, millions of people suddenly [have] to do something they have been discouraged from doing before: act for themselves, think for themselves, implement their innate creativity." After doing the work in this book, this will not be an issue for you. You are now aware that being wired for wisdom makes you able to find the answers to your life's queries. You are more able to adjust to the rapid change that surrounds you in today's world. By now I hope you have stopped asking yourself "How can I have it all?" and have started to ask "What do I really want?"—and my wish is that you are taking action accordingly. When you know what you want, you narrow the focus of your life to a portion that is manageable and where your success can breed more of itself.

You've probably noticed that I haven't delivered you to some magical nirvana. Nevertheless, I bet that you've started to experience magic, the magic of doing what feels right and of having your world respond positively. Satisfaction, happiness, fulfillment, and meaning need not be difficult to find. They are inherent to the wisdom you possess; you need only decide to have them and to make the wisest choices to protect them. You now have the tools to access that wisdom and therefore the meaning, satisfaction, and happiness you want.

It is up to you, however, to decide how hard you will make it for yourself. I used to believe that only three hours a day of aerobic exercise would give me the perfect body. Because I believed that, that is what it took. Now I believe that yoga, stretching, and meditation keep my body in ideal condition, and they do. I redirected the level of intensity of my exercise regimen from high impact to low impact, without giving up wonderful results. Similarly, you need to make a choice whether you will stay in the fray or find your satisfaction another way. I am not by any means suggesting your drop out or give up. Committing to living your best life means finding the speed and activity level that suits you, and then making the rest of your world cooperate in kind.

We live in an amazing time. A time when we are better off breaking the rules than keeping them. A time when we are free to design our lives based on our own wisdom without great fear of retribution. We are not called witches or radicals or hippies. Please take advantage of that. So many of the rules you live by are perceived expectations you have placed on yourself. Get out and be free. You hold the key to your own best life.

You've begun to think differently now. Give yourself permission to follow your own wisdom to your happiness. As your coach, I insist on it and will stand for nothing less. Be your own coach now, and accept nothing but the best for yourself.

Beware—it will change your life. Congratulations!

APPENDIX 1

MORE ON COACHING

WHETHER PEOPLE PAY FOR IT THEMSELVES OR THEIR COMPANIES FOOT the bill, more and more individuals these days are seeking out partnerships with professional coaches to get them where they want to go in their personal and professional lives.

Personal coaching is a service offered by a professional that uses advanced communication and life skills to help you create a successful personal and professional life. Some people use it to make life or career transitions, some to create more balance in their lives, others to upgrade existing businesses or goals, become better leaders, and still others as a way to absorb the constant change that surrounds them personally or at work.

The coach has become an evolutionary strategist. She asks people the questions that, as they answer them, will help them define their best life. She shows how to filter through information overload in order to glean the essentials people need to know to live well in today's world.

To find a coach, or to get more information on becoming one, contact one of the following:

Coach University
P.O. Box 25117
Colorado Springs, CO 80936-5117
800-48-COACH
www.coachu.com
Coach U is a coach-training organization that provides a referral service to locate an appropriate coach.

International Coach Federation
14441 I Street, N.W., Ste. 700
Washington, D.C. 20005-9039

888-423-3131 (main office)
888-236-9262 (coach referral service)
www.coachfederation.org
The largest nonprofit professional organization for the coaching profession. They have a referral service, information on all the coach-training organizations, and guidelines for attaining the PCC (Professional Coach Credential) and MCC (Master Coach Credential).

LBF•InterCoach, Inc.
26 Park Street, Suite 2045
Montclair, NJ 07042
888-23-COACH
973-857-8180
www.intercoach.com
This is Laura Berman Fortgang's coaching company, a resource for personal and executive coaching. All coaching is performed by coaches certified by the International Coach Federation and who ascribe to the techniques and philosophies put forth in Laura's books.

Clients include individuals and organizations such as:
The Army Corps of Engineers, TRICON, Prudential, Pharmacia, and Schering-Plough.

Other books by coaches:

Take Yourself to the Top: The Secrets of America's #1 Career Coach by Laura Berman Fortgang (Warner Books 1998)

Coach Yourself to Success: 101 Tips from a Personal Coach for Reaching Your Goals at Work and in Life by Talane Miedaner (NTC/Contemporary 2000)

The Portable Coach: 28 Surefire Strategies for Business and Personal Success by Thomas Leonard, Byron Larson (Scribner 1998)

Working Wisdom: Top 10 Lists for Improving Your Business by Thomas Leonard (Bard Press 1998)

Assess & Improve Your Company by John Seiffer (Decipher 2000)

Everyone's a Coach by Ken Blanchard, Don Shula (Zondervan Publishing House 1996)

Take Time for Your Life: A Personal Coach's Seven-Step Program for Creating the Life You Want by Cheryl Richardson (Broadway 1999)

Life Makeovers by Cheryl Richardson (Broadway 2000)

Co-Active Coaching: New Skills for Coaching People Toward Success in Work and Life by Laura Whitworth, Henry Kimsey-House, Phil Sandahl (Davies-Black 1998)

APPENDIX 2

WISDOM ACCESS

QUESTIONS

USE THESE WAQS FOR YOURSELF AND THE EXERCISES IN THE BOOK, and with your Life Blueprint group and people you interact with in your life.

What do you want?
What are you afraid of?
What is this costing you?
What are you attached to?
What is the dream?
What is the essence of the dream?
What is beyond this problem?
What is next?
What are you building toward?
What has to happen for you to feel successful?
What gift are you not being responsible for?

What are your healthy sources of energy?
What's stopping you?
What's in your way?
What would make the biggest difference?
What do you like to do?
What is right for you?
What do you hope to accomplish by having that conversation?
What do you hope to accomplish by doing that?

What's the first step?

What would it be like to experience the excitement and the fear at the same time?

What's important about that?

What would it take for you to treat yourself like your best client?

What benefit/payoff is there in the present situation?

What do you expect to have happen?

What's the ideal?

What's the ideal outcome?

What would it look like?

What's the truth?

What's the right action?

What are you going to do?

What's working for you?

What would you do differently?

What decision would you make from a position of strength?

What other choices do you have?

What do you really, really want?

What if there were no limits?

What haven't I asked that I should ask?

What needs to be said that has not been said?

What are you not saying?

What else do you have to say about that?

What is left to do to have this be complete?

What do you have invested in continuing to do it this way?

What is that?

What comes first?

What consequence are you avoiding?

What is the value you received from this meeting/conversation?

What is motivating you?

What has you hooked?

What is missing here?

What does that remind you of?

What do you suggest?

What is underneath that?

What is this person contributing to the quality of your life?
What is it that you are denying yourself right now?
What do you need to put in place to accomplish this?
What is the simplest solution here?
What would help you know I support this/you completely?
What happened?

What are you avoiding?
What is the worst that could happen?
What are you committed to?
What is your vision for yourself and the people around you?

What made you react this way?
What did you assume?
What have you learned?
What can you be grateful for here?
What is one thing you could do tomorrow?

What matters?
What matters now?
What matters most to you?
What anchors you?

What don't you want?
What if you knew?
What's your heart telling you?

What are you willing to give up?
What might you have done differently?
What are you not facing?
What does this feeling remind you of?

What would you do differently if you tapped into your own wisdom?
What does your soul say?

APPENDIX 3

RESOURCES

PART ONE. THE RECKONING

World Wide Online Mediation Center offers instruction & tapes: *www.meditationcenter.com*

To find a therapist: call 800-therapist (800-843-7274)

Alcoholics Anonymous: *www.alcoholics-anonymous.org*

National Sleep Foundation: *www.sleepfoundation.org*

National Committee for Quality Assurance (health care): *www.ncqa.org*

Healthfinder, a gateway website for health and human services from the United States government: *www.healthfinder.gov*

National Mental Health Association—call 800-969-6642 or go to: *www.nmha.org*

Books

Covey, Stephen R. *The 7 Habits of Highly Effective People: Powerful Lessons in Personal Change.* New York: Fireside, 1990.

Falter-Barns, Susanne. *How Much Joy Can You Stand: A Creative Guide to Facing Your Fears and Making Your Dreams Come True.* Rev. ed. New York: Ballantine/Wellspring, 2000.

Jeffers, Susan. *Feel the Fear and Do It Anyway.* New York: Fawcett Books, 1992.

Robbins, Anthony. *Awaken the Giant Within: How to Take Immediate Control of Your Mental, Emotional, Physical and Financial Destiny.* New York: Fireside, 1993.

———. *Unlimited Power: The New Science of Personal Achievement.* New York: Fireside, 1997.

PART TWO. THE DOING

National Association of Professional Organizers: *www.napo.net*

California Closets: *www.calclosets.com*

To avoid spam, contact Zero Junk Mail: call 888-970-junk or go to: *www .zerojunkmail.com*

Direct Marketing Associates (will remove your name from mailing lists). Write them at: Mail Preference Service, P.O. Box 9008, Farmingdale, NY 11735.

Maid Brigade—call 800-613-9856 or go to: *www.maidbrigade.com*

American Society of Interior Designers Referral Service: *www.interiors.org*

The Feng Shui Guild—call 303-442-8199 or go to: *www.fengshuiguild.com*

To search for homes in your area, go to: *www.realtor.com*

American Personal Chef Association: *www.personalchef.com/pclinks.htm*

Find information about alternative therapies at: *www.alternativedr.com*

To find a spa or getaway, go to: *www.spafinders.com*

To get insurance quotes, go to: *www.insuremarket.com*

Money/Financial

For financial advice and more go to the Motley Fool at: *www.fool.com*

Institute of Certified Financial Planners—call 800-322-4237 or go to: *www.icfp.org*

Credit Counseling Center of America—call 800-493-2222 or go to: *www.cpf-board.org*

American Institute of Certified Public Accountants: *www.aicpa.org*

For living trusts and wills, go to: *www.completetrusts.com*

Debt Counselors of America: *www.dca.org*

Debtors Anonymous: *www.debtorsanonymous.org*

Book

Orman, Suze. *The Nine Steps to Financial Freedom*. New York: Crown, 1997.

Career

The Internet Job Locator: *www.joblocator.com/jobs/*

New jobs are constantly being listed on monster.com. Go to: *www .monster.com*

CareerBuilder is a search engine that searches nearly all other Internet job sites. It also offers résumé help, interview, tips, etc. Go to: *www .careerbuilder.com*

Women.com has many career resources and other informative channels. Go to: *www.women.com/career*

PART THREE. THE BEING

Intuition Network: *www.intuition.org*

Intuition magazine online: *www.intuitionmagazine.com*

Books

Boorstein, Sylvia. *Don't Just Do Something, Sit There: A Mindfulness Retreat with Sylvia Boorstein.* San Francisco: HarperSanFrancisco, 1996.

———. *It's Easier Than You Think: The Buddhist Way to Happiness.* San Francisco: HarperSanFrancisco, 1997.

Chopra, Deepak. *The Seven Spiritual Laws of Success: A Practical Guide to the Fulfillment of Your Dreams.* Amber-Allen, 1995.

Choquette, Sonia. *The Psychic Pathway: A Workbook for Reawakening the Voice of Your Soul.* New York: Crown, 1999.

Day, Laura. *Practical Intuition: How to Harness the Power of Your Instinct and Make It Work for You.* New York: Broadway Books, 1997.

Franquemont, Sharon. *You Already Know What to Do: Ten Invitations to the Intuitive Life.* New York: Tarcher/Putnam, 1999.

Morgan, Marlo. *Mutant Message Down Under.* New York: HarperCollins, 1995.

Williamson, Marianne. *A Return to Love: Reflections on the Principles of a Course in Miracles.* New York: HarperCollins, 1996.

APPENDIX 4

FORMING YOUR OWN

LIFE BLUEPRINT GROUP

ᴹANY PEOPLE HAVE BEEN GATHERING IN GROUPS AROUND THE U.S. and abroad to work together on the Life Blueprint Process™ set forth in this book. If you would like to form your own group, we have collected what has worked well for other groups as a way to guide you. If you are curious about joining an existing group, there may be one in your area. Check out the Life Blueprint section at www.laurabermanfortgang.com for a list of existing groups, schedule of teleconference discussions, quizzes, study guides, and other resources.

Getting Started
Invite a group of like-minded people to join you:

- Gather friends like you would if you started a book club or study group in your own home.
- Ask your local bookseller if you can gather people at their store (they may even announce it in their newsletter or events calendar).
- Find some other workplace, community, or civic space that would be a good meeting place and ask others to join you.
- Make up a flyer (see website for a sample) and distribute it in your community.

Creating a Structure
As a leader, you get to create the group to suit you:

- Set an initial period of time that you would like people to commit to the process (i.e., once a week for a six-month period, once a month for a year).

- Decide the length of each meeting (probably determined by how many people are in your group).
- Ask people to choose a "buddy" to meet with in person or on the phone in between meetings for added support, discussion, and encouragement (accountability is important to your success with the program).
- Discuss ground rules for attendance, confidentiality, and how group members can address each other. Having a commitment from people to be present is important to the success of the group as well as people feeling safe to express themselves without worrying about the group gossiping with each other or with outside friends and family. Refrain from letting the group members talk at the same time and avoid telling others what they *should* do although suggestions are welcome.

Facilitating the Meetings
Being the leader doesn't mean being the expert; it means serving the group well. (Feel free to design this as you see fit):

- Let your first meeting be an introduction to each other, this book, and the procedures you intend to facilitate.
- Divide your meeting into two parts; the first is for discussion of topics and exercises, the second, for individual focus on people's own goals, growth, and change.
- Follow the chapters and exercises in order and announce a topic for each meeting at the prior meeting.
- Have each person choose an area of focus (something they are working on) for the duration of the process, i.e., career, life balance, relationships, money, finding meaningful work, etc. Your focus may change during the course of the process, but start with one thing you want to affect in your life.
- Assign homework. Let there be reading and exercises that need to happen in between meetings so each meeting can begin with discussion on people's progress.
- In the second part where participants are supporting each other individually, make sure everyone has equal time and attention. Draw out quiet participants by asking them what they think and help the more enthusiastic participants focus their energy on others as well as themselves.
- Use as many WAQs (Wisdom Access Questions) as possible when it is someone's turn to be helped with an issue.
- Have the group create a list of the resources they use in their life (lawyers, doctors, therapists, body workers, etc.) and distribute it to

the group so people can find what they need to succeed with their goals.

- Have some kind of ritual at the end of the meeting to help everyone wrap it up. Have people quickly go around the room and share a one-sentence nugget of what they are taking away from the evening's discussion. Or have people declare what they will do by the next time you meet or ask people to acknowledge each other for something that was done or said or discovered during the meeting.

Running a Successful Group

Please yourself and be sensitive to others:

- Accommodate and respect each member's pace.
- Allow the group to evolve to what naturally is the best format, pace, flavor, and focus.
- Be open to feedback.
- Don't bend to everyone's whims, but do acknowledge and take in all opinions and suggestions.
- Keep it light and fun. Growth is hard enough without the group taking itself too seriously.
- Keep an email list or call-chain system where changes in schedule, location, or just messages of encouragement can be sent.
- Celebrate a lot!

ACKNOWLEDGMENTS

THIS BOOK WOULD NOT BE POSSIBLE WITHOUT THE CLIENTS, SEMInar participants, keynote audiences, and newsletter readers who allow me the priviledge of working with them on their lives. Thank you for your trust and for being willing to share your experiences with me. It is a blessing to learn together.

Many people have been crucial to my success. Thank you to Patti Danos, my publicist, for your extraordinary care, brilliance, and ongoing support.

Thank you to the Blanchard family. I'm sure you don't even know it, but sharing this work with you gave it wings.

Carole Tonkinson, Eileen Campbell, and Megan Slyfield in the United Kingdom and the ever wonderful Mark Riminton—your support has been crucial to this project. Carole and Mark, you held the vision, and I finally feel the shoe fits. Thank you! And Carole, I appreciate your listening to me ramble as the germ of an idea became a strong concept for this book.

This book had many midwives on its way to life and I hope I don't miss anyone as I thank the rest. Thanks to Maggie Lichtenberg, who led me to her amazingly talented son, Greg Lichtenberg, whose support and tutelage are greatly appreciated. My thanks also to B. G. Dilworth, whose thoughts helped shape this project; Larissa Kostoff, for research; and a special thanks to Margaret Blackstone (Meg, Mego, Me with a G, MegHeart, et al.) for delivering me and this manuscript with love, dignity, and a gentle flair that only you can muster. Trent Duffy, you made it all sound good in the end.

Joelle Delbourgo, my wonderful agent, thank you for your enthusiasm, championship, and editorial insight on this project and on my career. Your style and grace throughout this process has been an inspiration.

Steve Sadicario at NSBienstock, thank you for making it fun to shoot for the stars. Your expertise and vision buoy me to keep going for the dream. Charles Keegan, your interest and commitment make it that much better, too.

To Wendy Hubbert, my editor, thank you. No author could ask for a more avid champion inside a publishing house. Thank you for taking this book to the top.

My thanks also to Susan Petersen Kennedy, Phyllis Grann, Nanscy Neiman Legette, Joel Fotinos, Ken Siman, Kelly Groves, Allison Sobel, Barbara O'Shea, Lisa Vitelli, Kristen Giorgio, Meredith Phebus, Claire Vaccaro, Diane Lomonaco, and the sales team at Penguin Putnam for your enthusiasm and your passion for my profession and my message.

In the coaching world, a big smooch of appreciation to Sandy and Melinda Vilas, owners of CoachU, Inc. Our joint love for this field has fueled a long partnership. Thanks for all you do for coaching and for me. Linda Miller, our conversation about guilt inspired passages in this book. Thomas Leonard, who put personal coaching on the map, thank you. And to all the coaches who have worked hard to forward this profession, I acknowledge you for your commitment to the work.

To the talented coaches at InterCoach—veteran member Susan Wallace, and Jeanne McLennan, Margaret Krigbaum, Corrine Luessing, Susan Corbett, Aboodi Shaby, Bill Ford, and Jackie Arnold—thank you for making me look good, doing great work with people, and making me laugh. And a special thanks to InterCoach vice-president Ellen Fredericks, without whom I would not have had the freedom to write this book and whose love and friendship are so precious to me.

To my assistant (read "wife"), Jeanne Bongo, thank you for thinking my thoughts, completing my tasks, and basically running my life when I can't. You are a godsend. And thank you to your family for their love of my boy.

There are so many friends and family who make up my circle of support that it is hard to thank you all individually, but please know your love does not go unnoticed. In particular, a hug and kiss to Madeleine Homan for always being there, D. J. Mitsch for holding me in the light that I sometimes forget to hold myself in, and Sheila Kutner for taking the ride with me. And thank you, Carolynn, for being my oldest and dearest.

To Fran and Bert, my mom and dad, my eyes swell with tears as I am filled with gratitude for your being here to share in the life I have made. Thanks for all your love, help, support, and baby-sitting. Thank you to Mort and Joan Fortgang, my in-laws, for loving us so and spoiling us rotten (and thanks for your baby-sitting, too).

To my husband, Mark: this book exists because you entered my life. Thank you for always believing in me and for being the wondrous soul who has partnered with me for the dance of life. And thanks for being a great dad to our guy and the babies. As hard as it is to leave home sometimes, it's comforting knowing they are all with you.

Skyler, thank you for coming into my life to make me wonder and discover it all over again. You are my best boy.

ABOUT THE AUTHOR

Laura Berman Fortgang is an internationally renowned speaker and the president and owner of InterCoach, Inc., a full-service coaching company devoted to supporting individuals, small businesses, and corporations to create extraordinary futures with less struggle.

Laura's work has allowed her to introduce the magic of coaching to diverse audiences from homemakers to Fortune 500 executives to NASA and the Army Corps of Engineers.

Laura is the author of *Take Yourself to the Top,* and her work has been featured nationally by *The Oprah Winfrey Show,* NBC's Weekend Today Show, and MSNBC, as well as in *Fast Company* magazine, *The Wall Street Journal, Redbook, Elle,* and *USA Today*. She was also the resident work/life coach for Women.com, where her weekly column and monthly work/life makeovers were seen by over five million visitors each month.

A founding member and veteran board member of the International Coach Federation, Laura has been influential in shaping the coaching profession worldwide and holds one of the first Master Coach Credentials granted by the ICF. She is currently on the board of Future Possibilities, Inc., a nonprofit organization delivering life skills training to children worldwide.

Laura resides in New Jersey with her husband and three children.

If you would like more information, care to subscribe to Laura's free on-line newsletter, "Living Wisely," or would like to form or join a Life Blueprint group, visit www.laurabermanfortgang.com.